The Way of Philosophy

The Way of Philosophy

AN INTRODUCTION

. . . . . .

CHAD ENGELLAND

CASCADE *Books* · Eugene, Oregon

THE WAY OF PHILOSOPHY
An Introduction

Cascade Books
An Imprint of Wipf and Stock Publishers
199 W. 8th Ave., Suite 3
Eugene, OR 97401

www.wipfandstock.com

ISBN 13: 978-1-4982-2096-5

Cataloging-in-Publication data:

Engelland, Chad.

    The way of philosophy : an introduction / Chad Engelland.

    x + 120 p. ; 21.5 cm—Includes bibliographical references.

    ISBN 13: 978-1-4982-2096-5

    1. Philosophy—Introductions. 2. Philosophy. 3. Conduct of life. 4. Values. 5. Wisdom. I. Title.

BD22 E64 2016

Manufactured in the USA

The quotation by Stephen Hawking is used courtesy of Guardian News & Media Ltd.

If you want to go down deep,
you do not need to travel far;
indeed, you don't have to leave
your most immediate surroundings.

—LUDWIG WITTGENSTEIN

Contents

Acknowledgments

Those whose conversations shaped this work include Damian Ference, Ron Hurl, Jeff Barnish, Ryan Mann, Kevin Klonowski, Patrick Schultz, Marty Dober, Elizabeth Barksdale, Abby Knapp, Brian Hula, and Francis Cavanna. The person who makes sure I do not lose sight of what is true, good, or beautiful is my wife, Isela.

1

Why Bother?

[Quest]

The first philosopher we know much of anything about, a fellow by the name of Socrates, proclaimed, "The unexamined life is not worth living."[1]

His statement hurt the feelings of his peers, who promptly put him to death. But Socrates didn't care about how people *felt*; he cared about how people *were*. And he thought most people were living life without really living. He loved them too much to stay silent: "Are you not ashamed of your eagerness to possess as much wealth, reputation and honors as possible, while you do not care for nor give thought to wisdom or truth, or the best possible state of your soul?"[2]

Our culture trains us to be superficial and shallow, to chase shadows and content ourselves with trifles. A look in the mirror tells us where that gets us: nowhere. We are empty inside. We are bored. We crave something, anything, we know not what.

What can we do? Socrates shows the way: go down deep with philosophy.

1. Plato, *Apology* 38a.
2. Ibid., 29e.

The Wonder of Life

Philosophy won't solve any of our problems. It won't, for instance, tell us how to land our dream job, attain our ideal weight, make lots of money, improve our self-esteem, or anything else that would be genuinely *useful*.

Perhaps philosophy is *entertaining*, then? I'm afraid not, which is why this book is not titled, *How Many Philosophers Does It Take to Screw in a Light Bulb?* While such a book would make for easy bathroom reading, it could not avoid giving the erroneous impression that philosophy itself is a joke, except one that isn't particularly funny.

If it is neither useful nor entertaining, what is the aim of philosophy? It wants to do nothing other than *provoke wonder*.

Wonder is neither useful nor useless, neither entertaining nor dull; it is something else altogether. Wonder fills us with unease, stinging us, numbing us, gripping us in the gut. But it also tingles and cajoles, hinting at something fantastic and exotic. It is this wonder that philosophers celebrate as the continual wellspring of philosophy itself, because it causes us to shed our conventional opinions and readies us to accept the truth. Wonder is awful and awesome at the same time. It rips us open to allow reality to fill us up.

Conventional wisdom lulls us into repose, but philosophical wonder is shock therapy. Wittgenstein writes, "Man has to awaken to wonder—and so perhaps do peoples. Science is a way of sending him to sleep again."[3] Philosophy awakens us to what is at stake in being human. Philosophy literally means love (*philia*) of wisdom (*sophia*), and it is the task of this little book to convey something of that love, something of that wonder of being confronted with the truth of things.

Most professional philosophers initially get interested in philosophy because they want to clarify properly human questions of meaning and purpose, but after a few years of studying philosophy they encounter all sorts of technical questions and puzzles, and

3. Wittgenstein, *Culture and Value*, 5.

they leave behind their original quest for meaning. (The older I get, the more I appreciate these puzzles. For example in the Liar's Paradox, a member of a set asserts that all members of the set are liars; so, a politician might call all politicians liars, but if they all are liars, and he is a politician, then he too must be a liar, suggesting he was lying about all politicians being liars. In philosophy, such logical puzzles abound.) Introductions to philosophy by professional philosophers typically present a host of technical puzzles that are interesting but somewhat removed from the wonder lying dormant in each of our hearts.

Boiled down to its essentials, this book introduces the nontechnical insights of the love of wisdom insofar as it clarifies what it means to live a meaningful and engaged life. That's it. No logical tricks, no mind-boggling inquiries into ultimate reality, no frightening suggestions that you might be a brain in a vat. These other questions are worth pursuing, but they have a power of distracting people from the question that naturally plagues us humans: what is this all about? This book outlines a path blazed by some of philosophy's greatest thinkers. Each section serves to make shine some key idea that illumines us on that way. The brighter they shine, the harder it is for us to persist in our repose, and the more likely it is that we will open our eyes and *wake up*. To this end, the book does mention a lot of philosophers that guide us into philosophy. A glossary lists a bit of information about each, including when they lived, and what sort of things they lived for.

Three Reasons to Philosophize

Why should we philosophize? I'll go with the weakest argument first because it is the easiest to follow. Some of the brightest of our species have devoted themselves to the pursuit, sacrificing lesser goods such as wealth and influence to the pursuit of wisdom. So, because Socrates, Plato, Aristotle, Marcus Aurelius, Augustine, Aquinas, Descartes, Kant, Kierkegaard, Thoreau, Nietzsche, and Wittgenstein, among others, have sought wisdom through philosophy, so should we. I said it is the weakest argument, because it appeals to authority. We are sensibly told to "question authority," but in truth we can't get by in life without it. Why should you get chemotherapy if you have cancer? Because the best doctors say so, not because you understand how it works yourself. You rely on their expertise and authority. Of course, if you happen to be a cancer doctor, you do not have to rely on authority; you know it for yourself. Similarly, if you are outside philosophy looking in, wondering, why bother, you should bother because those on the inside, who are the only ones in a position to know, say that you should come on in. Once you're in, you can judge the pursuit for yourself. The weakness is that just as the doctors could all be hacks, so the philosophers could all be fools. How can you judge someone's expertise when that's precisely what you yourself lack? Still, the aim of the argument is to motivate inquiry, not to give an irrefutable proof. There should be something contagious about the philosopher that makes you want to catch whatever he or she has.

The second argument is more complicated, but it is an ancient one. It goes like this: philosophy is unavoidable, because in order not to philosophize you have to philosophize. Say I didn't want to philosophize. I could argue that it was a pointless activity, because it was removed from life, led to endless questioning, or was incapable of arriving at the truth. But these reasons, given in behalf of avoiding philosophy, are themselves philosophical. To justify them, you would have to do a lot of philosophy; for starters, you'd have to clarify what life is about and what philosophy is, and only then would you be in position to justify the claim that they are divorced from one another. But all of this is honest philosophical work. Put simply: either you philosophize or to avoid philosophizing you still have to philosophize. The best approach, then, is to accept your fate rather than vainly seeking to avoid it. Philosophize, then. (Of course, you could just shrug your shoulders and turn over and go back to sleep; you've avoided philosophy through indifference, but you've also avoided using reason, which is proper to our species.)

The third argument is my favorite, because it is most personal and doesn't seem tricky. Why philosophize? Because we've got questions that we need to ask and nothing else can answer. So, I want to know what is the point of human existence, I want to know what I should do in a given situation, I want to know what the allure of beauty is, I want to know what happiness is. Physics, the queen of the sciences, naturally cannot answer such properly human questions, and it falls to the philosopher to tackle the really important questions we come hardwired with. Of all the animals, we are the unhappy, restless ones, who require so many things in order to grow and thrive. We are the most highly questionable animal, and when we question philosophically we awaken to what we are. Each of us, however attached we may be to passing delights, nonetheless hungers for something more, although we generally know not what. Philosophy lives this hunger intensely, ever on the scent of truth.

Incidentally, for those of you keeping track of such things, the first argument, from authority, can be found in Plato, who had been struck and wounded by the stunning figure of Socrates; the second argument, about the unavoidability of philosophy, is featured in an early work by Aristotle (and it came to ensnare Wittgenstein, who wanted to retire from philosophy but kept getting sucked back in); and the third argument, about human desire, can be found in any philosopher worth her salt. Descartes, for instance, rightly says, "The brute beasts, who have only their bodies to preserve, are continually occupied in looking for food to nourish them; but human beings, whose most important part is the mind, should devote their main efforts to the search for wisdom, which is the true food of the mind."[4]

Setting Aside One Reason Not to Philosophize

When my older sister came back from college on breaks, she brought philosophy books. At first I turned to them with unbridled

4. Descartes, *Principles of Philosophy*, 180.

enthusiasm, but I quickly grew discouraged when I discovered that philosophers generally disagree among themselves. Aristotle studied with Plato for twenty years but nonetheless disagreed with him in fundamental respects, and much later Descartes relegated Aristotle's followers to the cellar, and today it is extremely fashionable to think Descartes got just about everything wrong. Philosophers disagree, so philosophy appears impossibly difficult or quite doubtful.

To this objection let me make three remarks. First, philosophy is the passionate *pursuit* of wisdom—not its possession. Only Hegel claims to have achieved "Absolute Knowledge"; philosophers in the main claim a more humble, specifically human wisdom. In its beginning, philosophers insisted that gods do not philosophize, only human beings do. The founder of modern philosophy, Descartes, likewise remarks, "In truth it is only God who is perfectly wise, that is to say, who possesses complete knowledge of the truth of all things; but men can be said to possess more or less wisdom depending on how much knowledge they possess of the most important truths."[5] Our aim, then, is to achieve some progress in the path of human understanding, not to get everything right. Human beings understand the world from partial perspectives, and they consider different things in coming to a conclusion. A lot of disagreement is due to the limits of our own perspective and histories.

Second, this disagreement is good for philosophy. Much of what drives philosophy is very passionate disagreement with other philosophers, and philosophy is dead if it is seen as only a body of doctrine or set of ideas. Because philosophers disagree, we too must philosophize. If they all agreed, we might think we could somehow avoid the trouble of thinking for ourselves by memorizing their conclusions. But, as it is, no such avoidance is possible.

Third, amid all these profound differences, you would think a philosopher would despair, but an inkling of truth is all that is needed to fortify the flagging spirits and drive the philosopher

5. Ibid.

onward. Aristotle regards truth as a door hard to miss entirely.[6] We might err, for it is certain others have, but it is worth the risk, because something is at stake in human life, and philosophy is the only way to get at it. Is it impossibly difficult? There's no way to tell. Is it quite doubtful? Not necessarily. The only way to know for sure is to try it yourself.

Is Philosophy a Joke?

By most accounts, philosophy is utter foolishness. Its practitioners always appear slightly ridiculous. The first philosopher, Thales, nearly died while philosophizing. Plato relates the story: "They say Thales was studying the stars and gazing aloft, when he fell into a well; and a witty and amusing Thracian servant-girl made fun of him because, she said, he was wild to know about what was up in the sky but failed to see what was in front of him and under his feet. The same joke applies to all who spend their lives in philosophy."[7]

Philosophy usually occurs at a high degree of abstraction, but Plato crafted a vivid and memorable scene that engages the imagination. In the Allegory of the Cave, Plato asks us to consider the following situation.[8] In a dimly lit cave, a row of prisoners sits facing a wall. Chained in such a way that they can only face the wall ahead of them, they know nothing of the outside world or their own predicament. While their situation seems grim, they are perfectly content, because they are endlessly entertained by the images cast on the wall in front of them. For behind them are puppeteers who use an artificial light to cast shadows onto the wall in front of the prisoners. These moving images capture the attention of the prisoners, who spend their days talking about the entertainment. So engrossed are they that they hardly fathom a reality outside those images, outside the dim light of the cave. With this exotic scene, Plato wants us to awaken to our human

6. Aristotle, *Metaphysics* 2.1.

7. Plato, *Theaetetus* 174a.

8. Plato, *Republic* 514a–521c.

condition, for each of us is in the exact situation of the prisoners. How so? All of our views about life come from those who control the artificial light of entertainment. Think about how many hours of television and movies we've watched, how many hours we've spent listening to music and the radio. The world that we know and the opinions we have are rarely known by direct experience or careful consideration; mostly we have been fed views by script writers, directors, producers, marketers, politicians, and all those that control popular culture. Of course, much of what we learn in popular culture is right, but some of it goes horribly wrong. One of the jobs of philosophy is to flag some of the ideas of popular culture that muck things up.

What about Plato's prisoners? He asks us to imagine one being forcefully delivered from his bonds and turned around. As he looked away from the only reality he ever knew, he would at first merely grope about quite clumsily, hardly fathoming anything. Being shown the puppeteers, he would only slowly realize that they are the ones who provided the content to his whole worldview. Being led up out of the cave, he would be blinded and dazed, just as we are after a matinee when we leave a darkened theater. However, once his eyes adjusted to the daylight, he would see everything clearly; he would understand that the shadows cast on the wall find their truth here in the broad light of day. Now he is in the position to judge the truth and falsity of the views of culture, because he has access to the true reality of things. Philosophy begins with being unchained. It is confusing and bewildering at first, but once our eyes adjust, we can see things as they really are.

Now, suppose the liberated prisoner, having understood true reality as opposed to culture's shadows, were to head back down into the cave with the idea of telling other prisoners their predicament. His eyes having adjusted to the outside, he would be very slow at recognizing the shadows on the wall. Bumbling about, speaking of exotic insights, would he not appear perfectly ridiculous to them? All they know is the reality before them, and here someone who hardly seems expert in the very things they know so well claims there is something more, that something about the views they've been given is quite mistaken. Plato thought that this was the precarious position of philosophy and why, from the point of view of conventional wisdom, philosophy would always appear foolish.

Our culture is not all wrong, but in some fundamental and important respects, it is mistaken. The tradition of philosophy shows us a different path that leads up out of the cave and into the broad light of day. Philosophy can liberate us from what Bertrand Russell calls "the tyranny of custom."[9] Philosophers are unruly children who call it as they see it. If the emperor is naked even though everyone says he has clothes, the philosopher will blurt out the truth. In each section that follows I will argue that our culture's conventional view is only partially right and it is important for human life to make sure we get the whole truth. To live a properly human life, we need to be right about such key terms as truth, beauty, goodness, freedom, love, death, and the divine. If we're wrong about these, we will stumble about in the dark and are liable to go in circles. If we can gain some fundamental clarity about these guiding stars, however, we can hope to make some progress on life's way. Aristotle gets it right: "But unless one thinks one ought to endure living on any terms whatever, it is ridiculous not to suffer every toil and bestow every care to gain that kind of understanding which will know the truth."[10] Philosophy criticizes conventional ideas in order to bring to light just what it means to be human.

Is Socrates right that the unexamined life is not worth living? Nobody can answer this question for you. Rather, you are the one who must seek, think, and decide for yourself.

---

9. Russell, *Problems of Philosophy*, 157.
10. Aristotle, "Fragments," 2416.

2

Can Science Know Everything There Is to Know?

[Truth]

"Philosophy is dead," proclaims physicist Stephen Hawking.[1] He thinks philosophy has not kept up with the dizzying pace of scientific advancement, and it therefore falls to science to answer the deepest questions of the human heart. Hawking is surely right that the progress of science is impressive and yet hardly understood by most people. Scientists have conquered diseases, unraveled natural processes, and unleashed the forces of nature to allow us to fulfill our every fancy. No doubt still greater discoveries lie just over the horizon. Yet does this ability to manipulate nature mean that scientists are adept at philosophy? Can Hawking be right that scientists are on the verge of answering the most fundamental questions of human existence? While science is undoubtedly a wonderful human achievement, science cannot save each of us from the trouble of pursuing wisdom.

The closer scientists get to the most important questions, the more they forget the fact that they too are human, and we have to be wary of any account of being human that leaves out the fact that each of us happens to be one. Consider biologist Richard Dawkins, whose classic text, *The Selfish Gene*, provocatively

1. Hawking and Mlodinow, *Grand Design*, 5.

11

begins with a chapter titled, "Why Are People?" In the opening paragraph he dismisses as out of date every answer to that question from whatever source that was given prior to 1859, the year Darwin published *Origin of Species*. And what is his alternative? He ominously writes, "They are in you and in me; they created us, body and mind; and their preservation is the ultimate rationale for our existence. They have come a long way, those replicators. Now they go by the name of genes, and we are their survival machines."[2] The idea that the genes are selfish and that they programmed us is just a metaphor. In a new introduction, he quotes a reader who takes the view literally: "I largely blame *The Selfish Gene* for a series of bouts of depression I suffered from for more than a decade."[3] Rather than rein in the metaphor, however, Dawkins responds by saying, "If something is true, no amount of wishful thinking can undo it," and don't "shoot the messenger." At the same time, he points out sensibly that no "sane" person would remain with this "nihilistic pessimism." Instead, he says, "Our lives are ruled by all sorts of closer, warmer, human ambitions and perceptions." While Dawkins wants us to live with this contradiction between the scientific metaphor and the human reality, philosophy can dispel it. There is much more to life than meets the scientific eye, and philosophy gives us the means to take it seriously.

The philosopher Edmund Husserl expresses an admirably sensible attitude: "When science speaks we listen gladly and as disciples, but it is not always science that speaks when scientists are speaking."[4] *Scientism* is the name given to a view offered as science that is in fact armchair philosophizing. Science is good, but scientism is a great threat to the pursuit of wisdom. Under the guise of expertise, some scientists such as Dawkins obscure the meaningfulness of the human enterprise. They make a partial truth into the whole truth. In effect, they attempt to philosophize but can only do so badly.

2. Dawkins, *Selfish Gene*, 20.

3. Ibid., xiii.

4. Husserl, *Ideas I*, §20.

Scientists guilty of scientism make the philosophical claim, for instance, that science has proven that nothing besides brute matter exists. On this view, something like thinking about your grandma's recipe for apple pie can be explained in terms of basically material things, such as brains, genes, and the behavior of subatomic particles. These material things are causes of everything we experience, and they are the only things that really exist. However, the great discoveries of science do not support such a view. To see why, imagine the following situation. Sophia and Joshua go shopping at Walmart. Before they begin, they decide that only blue-colored products will go in their carts. Later, after exiting the store, they examine the contents of their carts and find, blue items. Would they be justified in inferring, from the results of their shopping, that there exist only blue items in the store? We've all been to Walmart and know that there are lots of red, yellow, green, and other-colored things for sale. Just because it's not on the shopping list doesn't mean it's not there in the store. But this is exactly the slip in reasoning made by many who popularize science. They reason that, since science only identifies material causes for things, there is nothing else to be found. But this does not follow. Rather, modern science wisely decides, as a methodological postulate, to specialize in material causality and ignore any other evidence and explanation. The fact that science only identifies material causes, then, is not an indication that there is nothing else to be found in reality but is merely the result of a previous methodological restriction. Each of us knows from our own experience that there are, so to speak, other things in the store: other good explanations beside scientific ones for why things are as they are.

The Evolution of Love

Every human being wants to be loved. The methods of science enable the scientist to discover the chemistry involved with love and to theorize about its evolutionary advantages. The scientific expert, however, goes beyond science and tells us that love is *nothing but* a chemical process, a mechanism of our evolutionary biology geared toward the transmission of genes. Every Valentine's Day the media happily report such things because they shock our sensibilities. The reason they shock us is because they bleach some of the most meaningful human experiences of personal worth and responsibility.

No philosopher denies that chemical processes and evolution affect us. But philosophers since Socrates have wondered about the *nothing but*—the claim that this is all there is. Science discovers the biology and chemistry of love, but it is pure ideology or scientism to say that the biology and chemistry provides the *complete account* of something like love. Can these reductive accounts make sense of a specifically human life?

The Athenians put Socrates to death because he was constantly questioning conventional wisdom and encouraging the pursuit of the inconvenient good. Just before he died, he said that science can get at the material structure of things, but it cannot answer the fundamental questions of life:

> If someone said that without bones and sinews and all such things, I should not be able to do what I decided, he would be right, but surely to say that they are the cause of what I do, and not that I have chosen the best course, even though I act with my mind, is to speak very lazily and carelessly. Imagine not being able to distinguish the real cause from that without which the cause would not be able to act as a cause. It is what the majority appear to do, like people groping in the dark; they call it a cause, thus giving it a name that does not belong to it.[5]

The known laws of physics and the particles in fields of force that exist are necessary *conditions* for Socrates's sitting in jail awaiting his execution. But they are not the sufficient *cause*, which is his decision to act for the sake of the good as he understood it. Matter is needed, but it is not the be-all and end-all of explanation.

5. Plato, *Phaedo* 99a–b.

Something else is more fundamental, and Socrates staked his life (and death) on it.

When we experience love, there are neurological processes occurring in our brains, hormonal elevations in our bloodstreams, and evolutionary advantages to reproduction. But this is only part of the picture. The most important ingredient is the meaningfulness of the activity. Do we rise above the mere animality of love and make it personal through virtue and vow, or do we let ourselves fall prey to anonymous processes? The personal is not reducible to the biological. The deadbeat dad, for instance, is not deficient in his biology. In fact, he may be far more successful in passing on his genes. Yet we know him to be deficient in his responsibility as a father. How do we account for this deficiency? Here, science cannot help us, but philosophy can. The failure is not biological, but personal; the father has transmitted genes, but he has not fulfilled the nature of human fatherhood and the responsibility it entails.

Why is responsibility so important for the personal? Nietzsche quips that humans are the animals that can make promises.[6] We're also able to keep them. We not only experience biological drives and emotional responses, but we can freely undertake to choose a course of action for ourselves. If my car breaks down, my plant does not bloom, or my dog runs away, I do not take it personally. But if a friend chooses to distance herself, I take it personally, because it is an issue undertaken deliberately. Even when the pheromones and oxytocin and emotional experiences are gone, we can still love through the free choice of our will. Human freedom does not show up on the scientific radar, but it is one of the key ingredients that makes meaningful a specifically human life. Love cannot be explained without talking about free will, and philosophy alone has the resources to do that.

6. Nietzsche, *Genealogy of Morals*, 493.

Thinking about the Brain

Due to everything we are learning about the brain, we can adopt a picture that tells us that we live "in" our brains, that somehow all our experience takes place within our skull casing. As Hawking puts it, "our brains interpret the input from our sensory organs by making a model of the outside world. We form mental concepts of our home, trees, other people, the electricity that flows from wall sockets, atoms, molecules, and other universes. *These concepts are the only reality we can know*."[7] But if we think about this for a second, we will be able to distinguish the genuine science from the bad picture we get if we misinterpret the findings of science.

How does the scientist know about what a brain does? Does he study his own through introspection? No, he cannot.[8] He can only study the brain of another: either the cadaver he dissects or the subject his equipment scans. What about these brain scans? How does he know what the subject is experiencing when different brain regions show activity? He must ask and listen to the human person whose brain he is scanning. The person in question knows what he is experiencing by experiencing it, *not* by looking at the brain scan. Further, the scan is a representation, not a photograph; it is more like a map than a satellite view. The representation maps where the blood flows, which is then interpreted as evidence of which parts of the brain are at work.[9] There is no direct experience of our brains. If we know anything about brains or anything else, that means we cannot be stuck inside our brains, and that means that there is more to thought than what our brains materially contribute. We cannot avoid the interpersonal world of life and love and language. It is impossible to be in the matrix or to be a "brain in a vat," because to be human means to be engaged with the things of the world along with our fellow humans.

7. Hawking an Mlodinow, *Grand Design*, 172 (italics added).

8. In a somewhat different context, the psychologist Steven Pinker observes, "Psychologists and neuroscientists don't study their own minds; they study someone else's" (*How the Mind Works*, 563).

9. See Noë, *Out of Our Heads*, 19–24.

The Achilles' heel of scientism is science itself. There exists science only where there are scientists, and there are scientists only where there are human beings open to truth. We cannot give a complete scientific account of things unless we give an account of scientists, and that means human beings open to truth. Can material causality give an account of openness to truth? We can cobble together an evolutionary account of human origins, the physics of energy available to our sense organs, the physiology of sensation, the neurology of the brain, the psychology of motivation, the economics of research, the sociology of professional societies, but in all these models you will not find an account of truth, since truth is *presupposed* by biology, physics, physiology, neurology, psychology, economics, sociology—in short, by science itself. These disciplines uncover truth*s* but not the nature of truth, which involves a peculiar transcendence of the human being. Only because scientists transcend nature can they ask questions and do science, and such transcendence exceeds the possibility of matter as scientifically conceived. Think about the equation, $2 + 2 = 4$. Even though your neural firings occur at a particular point in space-time, the proposition is not just true now but will be true in ten years as well. Scientific discoveries break free of the present to uncover truths that are timeless. How could matter explain this leap from space-time to timeless? Science cannot give a scientific account (and that means a *materialistic* account) of its own origins. As Heidegger puts it, "The existence of each natural scientist, as well as of each human being in general, always argues against their own theory."[10]

The difficulty does not stem from scientists but from ideologues who ignore their own rational activity and try to give an account of everything, science included, in terms of particles in fields of force obeying unyielding laws of nature. What they don't realize is that they saw off the branch on which they are sitting. Suppose you opened a fortune cookie that opined, "All fortune cookies are doubtful." Should you trust this fortune and therefore doubt all fortunes? But if you doubt all fortunes, must you not also

10. Heidegger, *Zollikon Seminars*, 198.

doubt this one that tells you to doubt all fortunes? Wisdom in this case would be to ignore the self-contradictory claim of the fortune cookie. Similarly, if modern natural science tells us we should have little confidence in our ability to know truth because we are brains processing nerve stimuli or machines engineered by our genes solely to reproduce, must we not also doubt this supposed truth? How can science discover truths about science, including the view that we are brains processing nerve stimuli or machines for reproduction, if, that is, we are in fact nothing but brains processing nerve stimuli or machines for reproduction? These beliefs are what philosophers call "self-defeating." They are beliefs that cannot possibility be true, because they implicitly deny their own truth. Like the politician who calls all politicians liars, or the fortune cookie that tells you to distrust all fortune cookies, the scientist who undermines our ability to grasp truth has undermined his ability to do science.

The facts of science are not facts of the neural network of the scientist's brain; they are facts about the publicly available world. They are not mere sensations—how things appear to me now—but they are individual aspects of truth. It falls to philosophy, with its special methods, to unpack such things. Science is equipped to describe the material basis of planets and molecules and thinking, but it cannot give a complete account of thinking, and it cannot give an account of truth, freedom, the human good, or even the activity of science itself. As Kierkegaard writes, "If the natural sciences had been developed in Socrates' day as they are now, all the sophists would have been scientists. One would have hung a microscope outside his shop in order to attract customers, and then would have had a sign painted saying: 'Learn and see through a giant microscope how a man thinks' (and on reading the advertisement Socrates would have said: 'that is how men who do not think behave')."[11] Accomplished scientists like Hawking and Dawkins who succumb to the ideology of scientism remind us again and

---

11. Kierkegaard, *Kierkegaard Anthology*, 430.

again of a truth observed by Heraclitus: "Much learning does not teach insight."[12] One can be learned while not being wise.

Is Truth Relative?

According to relativism, everything everyone believes is true. Of course, the view sounds immediately silly, since each of us knows that someone else is wrong about something and we've discovered we were wrong about something in the past. But the motive for holding such a silly view is complex. Relativism is on the rise today because our culture assumes that science can know all that there is to know. By consequence, if there is something that cannot be quantified according to scientific method, it is merely a matter of opinion, merely *relative*. In our political discourse, for instance, we try to figure out what we should do by taking opinion polls, because these can be quantified. We are completely at a loss about how to find the truth through reasoned discourse, so after circulating sound bites, we take a poll to decide what we are to do. Closer to home, mathematics and science cannot quantify questions of meaning and purpose. We agree to disagree about such things, taking them to be private matters of the heart. Philosophers, however, have very little stomach for such relativism, because it is incoherent. Plato points out that the relativist must believe that the person who thinks relativism is wrong is right: "In conceding the truth of the opinion of those who think him wrong, he is really admitting the falsity of his own opinion."[13] Relativism identifies appearance with reality, how things seem to each of us and how they are, but this leads to manifest contradictions. Two contradictory claims to truth cannot both be true. If one of us thinks something is round and the other person thinks it is square, at least one of us must be wrong. How can we decide between us?

Philosophy does not have telescopes and microscopes, it does not avail itself of mathematics and models, but it is not left with

12. Heraclitus, *Art and Thought of Heraclitus*, 37; translation modified.
13. Plato, *Theaetetus* 171b.

empty logic-chopping, for it has its own way of seeing. That is, philosophy grasps the nature of things. Science dissects to figure out how things work, but philosophy carefully considers *what things are*. When we achieve insight into the nature of a thing, we achieve insight into an unconventional truth, a truth that is not just someone's opinion, but is the truth of the matter. We cannot subject "freedom" to scientific analysis, but that doesn't mean anything goes. Philosophical method trains itself on the nature of such things and brings them to view. It does so first by contrasting them with things close to them (freedom seems like arbitrariness, but is it the same?) and then by determining which ingredients are necessary and which are not to make it the thing that it is (for instance, does freedom require reason, or can it get by without it?). Philosophy accesses things, then, by distinguishing one thing from another and sorting out essential and accidental features of things. Philosophers engage in such efforts not out of curiosity but out of wonder. For philosophy fails to forget what this is all about, and one of the key philosophical experiments to verify or refute a theory is to see if it stands up to the test of life. If the idea undermines existence and falsifies what is at stake, then it isn't worth much; if the idea allows us to get at the heart of life, then it is true. Philosophy has its own way of seeing, its own standards of reasoning, and its own way of experimenting.

Cultures that practice such abominations as cannibalism or female circumcision or infanticide are wrong to do so, and we can explain philosophically why they are wrong by appealing to the nature of the human being that is violated by such practices. The ideology of scientism, which rejects philosophy, leads to relativism about all such things. Dawkins, for example, soberly realizes that our decision to distinguish between the killing of a human and any other animal "has no proper basis in evolutionary biology."[14] Even though science cannot defend the ethical distinction between humans and other animals, philosophy can—as we'll see in the following chapters. While some matters, like our favorite colors or

14. Dawkins, *Selfish Gene*, 10.

artists, are merely relative, much of what science cannot know can yet be known by philosophy.

It presents no criticism of science if science cannot know all there is to know. It is geared toward repeatable material structures, but this does not include everything there is. Every inquiry has certain limits. Philosophy, for instance, is not capable of weighing in on the causes of disease or the interpretation of the fossil record, and a philosopher would be foolish to get upset if someone points out this limitation to her. I'll seriously consider what my doctor says about my health and my mechanic about my car, but I'll put little stock in what the doctor says about my car's clunking sound and what the mechanic says about the pain in my stomach. So should it be in this matter. Be suspicious of experts in biology, psychology, or the special sciences who pontificate about the meaning or meaninglessness of human life, but by all means listen to them about biology, psychology, or whatever is their area of expertise. Embrace science, spurn ideology, and seek wisdom.

No Pain, No Gain

Let's say I believe that a jolly fellow named Santa Claus exists and brings me presents. You tell me that in fact he is an elaborate ruse promoted by commercial ventures and continued by my parents and family. At first, I will be sad, no doubt. The truth will hurt. But imagine if no one told me. I would grow up thinking that Santa exists and brings me presents. Isn't my situation pitiable? Don't you have an obligation to remove the illusion and set me free for the truth? In the 1998 movie *The Truman Show*, Jim Carrey plays someone who grows up on a television show; all his family and friends are actors; he alone isn't. In real life, each of us is to a degree in the situation of Jim Carrey: not everything is as it seems. Not all our beliefs are true. Now even though our beliefs are to some degree false, we are free to act in our narrow world. But if we knew more of the truth, we would be to that degree freer to make meaningful use of our freedom. Jim Carrey, knowing the truth, courageously leaves the set to venture into the unknown but real world. Each of us on learning about Santa is free to quit bothering ourselves with strangers in Santa suits and to start focusing on more meaningful hopes and traditions. Truth makes free. We are only free to the extent to which we know the truth. Trapped in an error, we might feel fine, even good, but we are not really free. Therefore, if we care about each other, if we care about each other's freedom, we will care enough to share the truth as we see it, even when it hurts. In doing so, we ourselves have to face the possibility that we might be the ones wrong and unfree, but the only way to find out is to expose ourselves mutually to reasoned discourse about things, and then let the chips fall where they may.

Sometimes the truth does indeed hurt, but it is the kind of pain that accompanies growing up or growing strong, the kind of pain an athlete feels after a good workout. Suppose I believe that the meaning of life is to feel good, and I make all my choices with this end in view. You are my friend and realize that this belief of mine is false and is therefore a recipe for disaster. Rather than respect my wishes to avoid unpleasant talk, you kindly challenge me: "Where does pain fit into your philosophy? What about love and the sacrifice that it entails? Let's say I get really sick. Will your philosophy allow you to be with me in my pain? Will you visit me in the hospital when I am nearing death? If so, there is more to friendship than feeling good, and there must be more to life, too." Faced with the force of your argument, I see your point, and I change my view of the matter. Now that I have a better idea about life, I am free to make more meaningful choices. Incidentally, Augustine tells us that at one point in his life he suffered from this very confusion, although he later came to realize that friendship, not pleasure is what he really wanted.[15]

15. Augustine, *Confessions*, 5, 16, 26.

What Is Truth?

If truth is not a neurological process and if it is not relative, then what is it? Like all philosophical topics, truth is both obvious and slippery. We have to do considerable philosophical work to be able to understand what is right there in human experience, constantly resisting the temptation to make it into something else. Wittgenstein even resorts to imploring divine aid for the task: "May God give the philosopher insight into what lies in front of everyone's eyes."[16] Truth occurs when we bring ourselves into conformity with reality, when we allow beings to show themselves as they are. If I say, "The cat is on the mat," what I say is true only if and because the cat *is* on the mat. Reality determines what the truth is and not vice versa. Aristotle states this plainly as follows: "It is not because we think truly that you are pale, that you *are* pale, but because you are pale we who say this have the truth."[17] Truth, then, is not a psychological or chemical process, but it does involve our contribution, our presence to occur. Truth is not merely objective, but neither is it merely subjective or relative. A subject is required for its objectivity to occur. We human beings provide the place for things to reveal themselves. The equation $2 + 2 = 4$ would not exist if no one was around to think it, but the truth of the equation does not depend on the will or whim or biology of any subject. Even if you really want $2 + 2$ to equal 5, it never will. Moreover, when each of us correctly adds $2 + 2$ to get 4, there are indeed hidden neurons firing away in our heads, but the correct answer does not exist in our skulls; it exists for both of us together. The truth that the cat is on the mat is not a truth in your brain or mine; it is a truth "out there" concerning the relation of the cat and the mat, a truth that we have successfully registered. Truth, then, does not happen in our individual brains. Rather, it happens in the public interplay of mind and reality. We are the sort of living beings dynamically open to the truth of things. Truth can hurt because truth involves a dramatic encounter in which we bring ourselves into conformity

16. Wittgenstein, *Culture and Value*, 63; translation modified.

17. Aristotle, *Metaphysics* 9.10, 1051b7–9.

with the way the world really is. The adjustment can be painful even though it is always worthwhile.

Science wants to know everything, but wisdom concerns whatever is highest and best. As Nietzsche puts it: "Science rushes headlong, without selectivity, without 'taste,' at whatever is knowable, in the blind desire to know all at any cost. Philosophical thinking, on the other hand, is ever on the scent of those things which are most worth knowing, the great and the important insights."[18] Science overlooks the most important questions due to a curiosity about everything. Philosophy, by contrast, seizes upon the essential in wonder and becomes blind to the inessential. Plato writes, "It's ridiculous, isn't it, to strain every nerve to attain the utmost exactness and clarity about other things of little value and not to consider the most important things worthy of the greatest exactness?"[19]

18. Nietzsche, *Philosophy in the Tragic Age of the Greeks*, 43.
19. Plato, *Republic* 504d.

3

Is Beauty in the Eye of the Beholder?

[Beauty]

If we think about beauty—which we all do in our own way—we tend to say the following: *beauty is in the eye of the beholder*. In other words, it is merely subjective, merely an opinion or taste or preference that individuals have toward things, but it is no real feature of things themselves. Something or someone may appear beautiful to one person and ugly to another. I fancy this painting and you do not, but neither of us is "wrong." Every year, *People* magazine names someone the sexiest man alive. At most one woman is married to that man; the vast majority of women are married to someone else. What should these other women think of their own husbands? They can say sexy is in the eye of the beholder, not the beholden. One's woman's trash is another woman's treasure. But is this really what a wife wants to say? That her husband isn't *really* sexy, but only *seems so to her*? This is a critical point for human life and love. Let me put it pointedly: does each of us want to be loved because our lover merely *thinks* we are lovable, or do we want to be loved because we *are* lovable? In the former case, we are not loved at all; our lover just loves her subjective idea of us. And if beauty is in the eye of the beholder, then nothing is actually beautiful; nothing is really lovable.

Beauty is not merely subjective, but there is a subjective dimension that allows the objective dimension to shine through. Any husband really is sexy, no doubt, but often only his wife can appreciate that. Similarly, throwing a perfect game in baseball is a wonder to behold, but someone blind to the game's goodness would not appreciate it. Those who do appreciate the beauty of something tend to have an ability undeveloped in those who do not.

Arresting Beauty

When we think about beauty, we tend to say it is merely a matter of opinion, but that is not how we act or respond when we encounter beauty. Beauty calls to us, and it grabs our attention. Advertisers know this. Products are linked with beautiful people and sometimes disappear behind them. Beauty captures our attention and changes our behavior. More personally, the very glimpse of a beautiful member of the opposite sex can fundamentally alter our life, causing us in a short period to realign our priorities and begin a life of sacrifice for her or him. Beauty can change us to our core. Therefore, it cannot be merely an opinion or a taste. Instead there is something more here.

We think of beauty as something harmless, but beauty is extremely powerful. Beauty breaks in upon the ordinary hum of our lives. We do not stop to smell the roses, but instead the roses stop us. They capture our attention and arrest our activity if we but let them. Beauty shows itself as a call, as a summons, not something that is merely in the eye of the beholder.

The experience of beauty is puzzling. It overwhelms us and makes demands on us, but just what is its demand? Plato experienced the power and perplexity of beauty more than any other philosopher. He compares the experience to a child teething, overcome both with pain and yet a sense of promise. Beauty, he says, arouses a demanding love in us, and each one of us, to the last man, woman, and child, loves happiness. For Plato, beauty is the clue for just what happiness might mean in human life. At the summit of his philosophical speculation, Plato unpacks the meaning of beauty and thus the meaning of love: "In the presence of beauty, love wants to give birth both in body and in soul."[1] At the heart of beauty and love is a desire to be fruitful and creative.

The poet, for instance, experiences the beauty of nature or the beauty of the beloved and gives birth to poetry: "O, how much more doth beauty beauteous seem / By that sweet ornament which truth doth give! / The rose looks fair, but fairer we it deem / For that sweet odour which doth in it live."[2] Nor is such fruitfulness the special provenance of the poet. It is what continually nourishes new scientific theories. Charles Darwin, for instance, concludes his magisterial *Origin of Species* by emphasizing the beauty of living form: "There is grandeur in this view of life, with its several powers, having been originally breathed by the Creator into a few forms or into one; and that, whilst this planet has gone cycling on according to the fixed law of gravity, from so simple a beginning endless forms most beautiful and most wonderful have been, and are being evolved."[3] Albert Einstein finds the encounter with mystery to be supremely beautiful: "The most beautiful experience we can have is the mysterious. It is the fundamental emotion that stands at the cradle of true art and true science."[4]

In everyday life, too, beauty arrests us and arouses us and invites us to be fruitful. We witness a half-court shot at the buzzer and shout for joy; overcome by beauty, we forge a life together with our spouse and bring forth children into the world, children that we not only clothe but educate as to the meaning of beauty, the meaning of life. Plato thinks that each of us lives on in whatever we bring into the world through beauty: children, poems, theories, or memorable moments.

1. Plato, *Symposium* 206b; translation modified.
2. Shakespeare, *Love Sonnets*, Sonnet 54.
3. Darwin, *Origin of Species*, 243.
4. Einstein, "World as I See It," 11.

The Beauty of Being Human

What is beautiful? When we behold the sunset, the extraordinary pinks and purples splashed across the sky fill us with awe. The rhythm and melody of music transport us into a different mood and tempo. Encountering anything beautiful, anything clothed with an elegant form or suggesting a powerful depth, we shudder as before something holy and treasured. Wittgenstein invites us to consider the objectivity of beauty: "Suppose someone were to say: 'Imagine this butterfly exactly as it is, but ugly instead of beautiful'?!"[5] If you can't imagine the exact same butterfly as ugly instead of as beautiful, then beauty must not be something you impose on things but must be a feature of things. Someone who didn't find the Grand Canyon beautiful would be someone out of tune with what is there. The beauty of a thing is in the thing beheld, not in the one beholding. But do we see things as they really are?

All around us are different kinds of energy, but we have evolved organs to pick up only a narrow range of visual and auditory information. Some animals see and hear more, and still others experience different ways of perception. Think of bats, which echolocate, finding their way about by a kind of radar. Certainly, we could have evolved a completely different set of organs that would have, for instance, allowed us to directly experience radio waves without having to translate them into sound waves, or to directly perceive thermal energy and nuclear energy instead of needing instruments that translate these into our visual and auditory fields. The point is that we could see and experience beautiful things, with their form and depth, quite differently had we different organs, and there does not seem to be any necessity to our having the particular organs that we do have. Is beauty merely something subjective, due not only to our personal preferences but even to the peculiarity of our sense organs?

The experience of the beauty of things is not merely subjective even though we could conceivably perceive things in a radically different way. How is that? Our sense organs allow the beauty

5. Wittgenstein, *Zettel*, §199.

of things to be revealed through their visual and auditory qualities. Were we to have evolved different organs, we would be closed to the beauty of these dimensions, but we would be open to the beauty of different dimensions. Our sense organs do not impose beauty on things; rather they allow the beauty proper to things as they are in a field of energy to be manifest in one way or another.

It does not matter much what kind of sense organs we have, for our human ability to understand and to speak could have made use of other ways that things appear. What is essential, then, is not the peculiar way things appear in their beauty, but the very fact that things are beautiful, and the fact that we to whom things are beautiful have a unique nature, one that can appreciate them. Heidegger poetically calls us "shepherds of being," because we have evolved to be the ones to whom things are intelligible, and that means beautiful. Augustine says, "Animals, both small and large, see the beauty, but they are not able to question it, for in them reason does not hold sway as judge over the reports of the senses."[6] Beauty, then, tells us not only about things but also about ourselves as the ones filled with awe before beautiful things, as the ones moved by the experience of beauty.

The Beautiful Game

We often hear about the importance of role models for children to imitate, and we grimace when our celebrities live lives that are not a pleasure to behold. When we do not look for our models among Hollywood stars and NBA players but look closer to home, we can discover a truth philosophers have cherished: being good is beautiful. Being a good mother or father, being a good doctor or lawyer, being a good chef or mechanic, has a luster and sheen. There is glory in these very rare things, and when we have the pleasure of witnessing them, we are moved by their beauty. Plotinus puts it this way: "Seeing of this sort is done only with the eye of the soul. And, seeing thus, one undergoes a joy, a wonder, and a distress

6. Augustine, *Confessions*, 10, 6, 10.

more deep than any other because here one touches truth."[7] A mother who skillfully calms an upset child, redirecting his attention toward his genuine good, exhibits a grace and beauty. A meal made with care, competence, and creativity delights and gives joy.

We call soccer "the beautiful game," because it unites us and draws us out of our everyday concerns. In a larger sense, life itself is the beautiful game. Beauty gives rise to joyful contemplation and reveals the goodness of life. We are pulled out of the thick of things to experience the goodness of things. In the presence of beauty, we feel that it is good to be here. Similarly, when we love someone, we feel it is good that they are here with us. We experience the objective beauty and goodness of a person in his or her particularity. Love allows us to see what is really there.

The idea that *beauty is in the eye of the beholder* is unlivable. It expresses a lazy way of thinking in which something is either purely objective, like a rock sitting before us, or purely subjective, like one's favorite color. Beauty is objective, but it elicits a subjective response and requires a subjective openness. We need an eye for beauty in order to let it transform us. The call of beauty offers us an opportunity. We can contemplate it and allow it to multiply in our own lives, or we can let the opportunity pass us by. When we give ourselves over to it, it makes us better by arousing in us a desire to love and be lovable.

7. Plotinus, *The Essential Plotinus*, 37–38.

4

If It Feels Good, Why not Do It?

[Goodness]

Imagine a time in the not so distant future when virtual reality technology advances to the point where the virtual world is just as vivid as the real one. Now imagine that in this virtual world, though not in the real world, all your hopes, dreams, wants, fantasies, and whims are instantaneously met. You want a gourmet meal, you want romance, you want to be rich and powerful . . . it is immediately fulfilled. With all these sensual, erotic, and social successes you would presumably feel great, but would you be happy?

Perhaps this thought experiment is too fantastical. Imagine this alternative. In the not so distant future, a pharmaceutical company develops a little pill with no side effects. Popping the pill makes you feel great no matter what your circumstances.[1] If you just take the pill, every day you would experience unmitigated euphoria, but would you be happy?

To answer this question, we have to ask what might seem to be a silly question: what is happiness? Everyone wants to be happy, but there is some confusion regarding just what happiness is. In conventional usage, happiness suggests a passing feeling or mood that *happens* to us. We feed children McDonald's Happy Meals. We

1. Novelist Aldous Huxley envisions just such a pill (*Brave New World*, 261).

31

teach them to sing the song, "If You're Happy and You Know It," and the singing and the clapping infectiously make them feel good. If we are sad, a friend will try to make us happy by cheering us up. We pepper our written messages with smiley faces and emoticons to spread the cheer. When somebody does something we wouldn't, we say, "Well, whatever makes him happy." If this is what happiness means—feeling good—then having a life of perfect pleasure would seemingly make us happy. But is this all there is to happiness?

Philosophers don't think so. In fact, Plato says that victory over pleasure is the "noblest of all." He adds, "If they win this battle, they'll have a happy life—but so much the worse for them if they lose."[2] The idea of a battle suggests a dangerous foe. Why might the greatest philosopher of all time think pleasure is our *enemy* in the quest for happiness?

First, pleasure disappoints. We seek it, thinking it will fulfill us, but instead we find that it is fleeting and that the enjoyment falls short of our desire. The doughnut looks tastier than it is.

Second, pleasure enslaves. The more we give ourselves over to it, the more we want it, and the more desperate does our desire for it become. We can start thinking of doughnuts all the time and start coming up with excuses to have doughnuts around.

Third, pleasure can mislead us. Even though doughnuts taste good, it turns out they are not terribly good for us, because in immoderate quantities they tend to make us sick in the short term and fat in the long term.

Fourth, pleasure retards our development. Pleasure is enjoyed in the present moment. But to grow involves changing in the present for the sake of some future good. In order to be healthy tomorrow, for example, I might want to forgo today's doughnut buffet and instead eat some fruit and go for a run. This may not seem as pleasant in the short term, but it better serves our good. To want to grow means we work for a future good and do not let ourselves be tyrannized by the present moment.

---

2. Plato, *Laws* 840c.

Plato highlights another reason a purely subjective sense of happiness fails. Serial killers presumably delight in their killing, which we can safely say is objectively bad. They very well might feel good, but they are undoubtedly not flourishing. Our usual subjective view—whatever makes him happy—is clearly inadequate. Pleasure is peculiar, because even if we seek it as our end, we always have to do something in order to achieve it: we have to pop a pill, have sex, watch a TV program, or do a virtuous action. What makes the pleasure good or bad, then, is the kind of activity it attaches to.

I am told that most puppies will overeat if given the opportunity and that in some cases overeating can lead to bloating and even death. Dog owners must strictly regulate portions for the sake of the puppies. We are like those puppies. There is no natural limit to our desire for pleasure. If we try to take in as much as we want, we will make ourselves miserable. That's why parents should not give in to every whim of their children, nor should they give in to every whim in themselves. Instead, they should take their pleasure in due proportions, just like well-cared-for puppies.

If happiness is not feeling good, what is it? The sight of a puppy or a child indulging itself to the point of harm is sickening, but it is no less sickening when we the adults are doing so with our own pleasures. By contrast, a well-trained puppy or a well-raised child or a self-controlled adult is beautiful to behold. Happiness is a beautiful state of flourishing or objective well-being. A happy person is one who is an exemplary human being, one who realizes the full meaning of being human. If and only if we conquer pleasure will we be happy.

Three Kinds of Friendship

Today on the social network Facebook we can friend and unfriend with ease, making it possible to have hundreds of friends at once. But according to Aristotle, true friendship is extremely difficult to achieve and extremely rare. We might have a couple of such friends in our whole lives. In books 8 and 9 of the *Nicomachean*

Ethics, Aristotle classically describes three kinds of friendships based on three grades of goodness. There is the goodness of pleasure, the goodness of utility, and the goodness of virtue. In a friendship founded on *pleasure*, each of the friends seeks pleasure from the other; for instance, a person might be funny or fun, and if the person stops being funny or fun, a friend who values the pleasure of friendship would stop hanging out with the person. Such friendships are especially frequent among young people. In a friendship founded on *utility*, each of the friends seeks something useful from the other; one might befriend a mechanic, but when he retires the friendship will cease. These friendships are especially frequent for older people. With both pleasant and useful friendships, one does not so much seek the good of the other as what one can get out of the relationship. Jim befriends Ava because he feels good when he is around her, or he befriends Stephen because he has a lot of connections that may prove beneficial. Very likely Ava and Stephen are seeking the same things from Jim. Rather than simply willing the good of the other person, then, Jim wills his own good (pleasure or utility) through the other as the reason for the friendship: "I'll scratch your back, *if* you scratch mine."

It is otherwise in a friendship founded on *virtue*. Each of the friends delights in the very goodness of the other. Ava does not seek to get something from Stephen, and Stephen does not seek to get something from Ava. They are not "friends with benefits." Rather, they enjoy the very goodness of each other, and they take the good of the other person as their own good. Of course, such friendships will be pleasant and useful too, but these are not the reasons for the friendship. If something bad happens to Ava, Stephen will be there to help; even though Ava is grouchy and no longer useful, he still regards her good as his own. There is a kind of stability and permanence to this most rare and treasured form of friendship. Because each friend wills the good of the other, the friends will correct each other when they are wrong. Descartes says of such friends, "We desire praise from those who do not know us, but from friends we want the truth."[3] What is so special about virtue that it enables the best kind of friendship?

The Crown of Virtue

A hallowed New Year's tradition has us try to reform our lives and drop our bad habits, but as most of us experience, those habits are really, really hard to shake. We give up eating sweets, but find ourselves with the hand in the cookie jar one week later. We give up swearing, but find ourselves still swearing. We try to throw off an addiction but cannot resist its craving. If we are free beings, endowed with wills, why can't we just decide not to do something anymore? Why do those habits exercise such power over us?

Habits establish a kind of momentum in us. We are bodily beings, and our bodies record and retain the movements we give them. If we stand at the free throw line every day at practice, sending up ball after ball, it eventually becomes easier to make the shot. If we practice the piano day after day, it becomes easier to play. Habits give us a kind of second nature, an ease and expertise in doing something. Virtues are so important because they are habits that give us an ease and expertise in acting well.

Four virtues in particular are crucial for human flourishing, and they are accordingly called the "cardinal" or hinge virtues. These four are habituated ways for relating to some aspect of life. *Moderation* enables us to relate rightly to pleasure, *courage* to relate rightly to pain, *justice* to relate rightly to other people, and prudence or *wisdom* to relate rightly to the truth.

Moderation

We have to wonder just what kind of role model Sesame Street creators thought Cookie Monster would be for children. That furry blue beast, avidly eating everything in sight, vividly portrays the excess to which every child is prone. And it is not just children

3. Descartes, "Early Writings," 4.

who lust after pleasures, grasping for candy and cookies and having meltdowns when they don't get want they want. Adults have the same desire for pleasure but with the added complication that the palette for pleasures has grown much, much wider (and more expensive). If an unbounded appetite for pleasures plunges us into monstrous madness, moderation helps us regain our sanity. Pleasure has an allure, but moderation takes control. It does not deny the goodness of pleasure, but it also does not think pleasure is the only or even the highest good. Moderation allows us to enjoy pleasures without harm to ourselves and others. It realizes that the desire for pleasure knows no bounds and would readily make us subject to its wants. Moderation, then, keeps us free in relation to passions that would easily enslave us in self-destructive addictions and habits. The "no" issued by moderation is the flipside of a "yes" to freedom and the authentic good. But moderation is not only useful. It also ennobles and beautifies behavior. Instead of monsters, we look like humans.

In a famous psychological experiment, four-year-olds were given one marshmallow by researchers and told they could have another if they waited fifteen minutes before eating it.[4] The researchers then left the room while the camera recorded. Some of the children ate the marshmallow right away; others, obviously distraught, fidgeted about before eating it; and a few waited the whole time. The ability to delay gratification turned out to be a more accurate indicator of long-term school performance than the child's IQ. The children who could wait exhibited self-mastery, which transferred to success on a host of other issues. All the children wanted the marshmallows equally, but the delayers were able to turn their attention to other things. The significance of the marshmallow experiment for human happiness is not that the ability to delay gratification can lead to more gratification. Rather, the ability to control the desire for pleasure is a principal attribute of being a successful human being.

4. Shoda et al., "Predicting Adolescent Cognitive and Self-Regulatory Competencies," 978–86.

Immanuel Kant speculates that the ability to refuse urges for pleasure is the very factor that in prehistoric times ushered in a properly human existence: "Mere animal desire was gradually converted to love and, with this, the feeling of mere pleasure was converted to a taste for beauty, initially only in the human being, but then also in nature."[5] Animals move according to instincts, but the ingredient of human freedom, which can moderate and direct animal urges, makes possible a realm of interpersonal love and an eye for beauty.

In the *Phaedrus*, Plato provides a memorable image for moderation. He asks us to consider the soul as a chariot drawn by two horses.[6] The charioteer represents our reason, and the horses represent two kinds of passions. One horse is ugly, base, impulsive, and obstinate. The other horse is beautiful, noble, strong, and obedient. At the sight of someone attractive, the base horse immediately lurches forward, intensely struggling to drag the chariot with it. The charioteer is caught off guard, and the chariot rushes forward in hot pursuit. The charioteer can come to his senses and pull on the reins, attempting to drag the base horse to the ground, but he has little hope of success if he does not have the noble horse as his ally. For the noble horse alone can be trained to listen to the commands of the charioteer, but the base horse must simply be beaten. Plato's point is that moderation makes an ally of our passion for nobility in order to restrain and beautify our unruly appetite for pleasure. Without such an ally, we might know what we should do, but we will lack the resolve and the resources to do it. Moderation makes an ally of the beautiful horse to help us on the way.

In our technological and consumerist society, one of the most important kinds of moderation is *simplicity*. Our desire for new things is completely insatiable. The error of consumerism is to give in to this want, to think that our happiness is to be found there. Rousseau argues, on the contrary, that technological conveniences

5. Kant, "Conjectural Beginning of Human History," 27.
6. Plato, *Phaedrus* 253c–254e.

do not satisfy us: "For in addition to their continuing thus to soften body and mind (those conveniences having through habit lost almost all their pleasure, and being at the same time degenerated into true needs), being deprived of them became much more cruel than possessing them was sweet; and they were unhappy about losing them without being happy about possessing them."[7] A new gadget makes us feel good for a week and then we grow accustomed to it, and we have more sorrow when it breaks down than we had joy when it was working. In other words, the multiplication of our technological devices, acquired to make us feel good, only makes that feeling more and more precarious. By contrast, simplicity looks for fulfillment apart from gadgetry. Thoreau, an American, notes that philosophers embrace simplicity as the outward clothing for their inward wealth: "With respect to luxuries and comforts, the wisest have ever lived a more simple and meager life than the poor. The ancient philosophers, Chinese, Hindoo, Persian, and Greek, were a class than which none has been poorer in outward riches, none so rich in inward."[8] Thoreau wisely sought to live simply and thus richly, too.

Courage

We usually associate courage with heroic actions on the battlefield or in freak occurrences. (Think of the fellow who jumped onto the subway track to save someone having a seizure just as a train bore down on him.[9]) Courage is also an everyday virtue. Each of us, whatever our situation, has an opportunity to exercise it.

Courage is that virtue that masters fear of pain, just as moderation is that virtue that masters desire for pleasure. Why is mastery needed? Because avoiding pain is not always the best course of action. If we shrink from every challenge for fear of pain, we will wither away and withdraw from every opportunity for greatness.

7. Rousseau, *Discourse on the Origin of Inequality*, 48.

8. Thoreau, *Walden*, 12.

9 Buckley, "Man Is Rescued by Stranger on Subway Tracks."

To flourish, we have to master our natural aversion to pain so that we can choose the good even if it requires suffering. Now, the ultimate painful thing is death, which is why acts that risk the pain of death for some noble good are especially courageous. The soldier and the hero risk death in view of the nobility of the end. One's homeland or the life of a victim is worth the risk. In effect, courage declares, "This risk or suffering is necessary, and therefore I willingly accept it." Between cowardice, which fails to act because of fear, and recklessness, which merely ignores fear, courage knowingly faces a fearsome situation and acts as is needed. Hope, not fear, moves it. Courage makes us free because it masters a strong impulse in us—our impulse to avoid pain—and so allows us to pursue our genuine good.

In a special way, suffering seems to slow down the passage of time. While pleasure collapses time into the present moment so that we forget the future, pain nails us to the present so we almost despair of the future. Courage releases us from the tyranny of the present, and when it does so we call it *patience*. Courage by this name has us endure the aggravations of life, such as unpleasant coworkers, bad drivers, and sickness. The danger is that we would break down and lose ourselves. Courage masters the threat because it remains aware of what our good really is. It keeps the proper perspective on the situation, and that is everything: for the tyranny of the present annoyance lies precisely in its complete lack of perspective, in its insistence that somehow it is the only thing that really matters. The trials and tribulations of everyday life continually threaten to break us, but courage as patience nobly endures what needs to be endured.

Courage also expresses itself as *fidelity* to our promises and vows. Now, we make a vow in view of the certain difficulty of the task and the fickleness of our impulses and feelings. Fidelity takes a good deal of courage; even in the midst of suffering, it chooses to remain true to oneself, one's vow, and one's responsibilities. A president faithfully upholds the Constitution even when it would be easier to circumvent it. A spouse remains faithful even when it would be more pleasurable to cheat. There is courage in taking the more difficult but more noble route.

Courage takes a variety of shapes. The fight against the many forms of injustice is one that likewise requires courage, patience, and fidelity. For injustice generally has power on its side, and engaging it therefore involves risk, suffering, and a real commitment. The pursuit of philosophy likewise requires courage, for we must be ready to lay down our beliefs, however cherished, if they turn out to be false and life-denying. Wittgenstein says, "You could attach prices to thoughts. Some cost a lot, some a little. And how does one pay for thoughts? The answer, I think, is: with courage."[10]

Justice

The virtue of justice governs our relationships with others. The difficulty in being just is controlling our own tendencies to seek our private advantage at the expense of others. The Golden Rule counters the tendency to outdo others by counseling us to do to others as we would have them do to us. It jolts us out of our own perspective, and invites us to take up the perspective of others. In the Categorical Imperative, Kant formulates the rule more positively: treat others as ends, not as means.[11] We must acknowledge that others are people too, and we must treat them as such. This means we do not use them for our own advantage. Instead, we must act in such a way that we would will that every human being would act in the same way as we do. If everybody cheated, cheating would never work, because trust, which makes cheating possible, would be destroyed. If we all acted like greedy Wall Street executives, our economic system would collapse, which would be bad for everybody, even greedy Wall Street executives. At the same time, justice is not some cold minimum of behavior. Thomas

10. Wittgenstein, *Culture and Value*, 52.

11. "Act in such a way that you treat humanity, whether in your own person or in the person of another, always at the same time as an end and never simply as a means" (Kant, *Grounding for the Metaphysics of Morals*, 36).

Aquinas says we are obliged in justice to be friendly toward everybody we encounter.[12]

We say we try to keep up with the Joneses, but really we try to outdo them. It is not enough to match purchase with purchase, novel item with novel item, luxury with luxury, success with success, but in truth we want to be the ones pulling ahead in the competition. Only there is no competition. Rousseau rightly singles out living in the eyes of others as one of the great vices to which modern life is especially prone.[13] Doing things simply to be noticed is to be a slave to superficiality. Recognizing this tendency of the human heart, Plato sketches an alternative to the endless quest to outdo others. Instead of seeking our own advantage in everything, we can contribute to the common good. When I am sick I go to the doctor not because I want to give him money but because I want to be healed. The doctor wants to be paid for his services, and he deserves to be paid for his services, because he has in fact done a good for me. Plato's argument, then, is that the doctor does not simply seek his own advantage: he does good to the patient and therefore derives monetary gain. He contributes to the common good and therefore derives private advantage. Suppose, however, that he was not interested in the good of the patient, but only in monetary gain. Let's say he ordered unnecessary tests and prescribed unnecessary drugs. Then, he might get what he wanted, but he would sacrifice the satisfaction of being a good doctor; he derives his private advantage at the expense of his objective goodness.

Consider another example. It is the job of "flavorists" to flavor processed foods like soft drinks and potato chips. Since tasty food is a good for the consumer, flavorists contribute to the common good and are justly paid for their efforts. Suppose, however, some flavorists decide to make a food addictive instead of satisfying. They engineer it to have an initial explosion of flavor that quickly fades so that consumers hanker for more. That is, indeed, how

12. Aquinas, *Summa Theologiae*, II–II, q. 114, a. 2.

13. Rousseau, *Discourse on the Origin of Inequality*, 70.

two flavorists described their aim to CBS's Morley Safer. They said they wanted a powerful beginning and an unsatisfying end so that people will hunger for another bite.[14] What eater wants to eat food that frustrates instead of satisfies? Consumers deserve tasty *and* satisfying food, but in this case they are being used as mere means to the end of making money. Such an aim violates justice and goes counter to the common good.

The common good, then, is the great Platonic alternative to the axiom that might makes right. The communal good and not private advantage provides the domain for human flourishing. It recognizes the dignity of each human being, preventing each from being mere means to an end. It seeks the development of society as a whole, recognizing that the most satisfying human goods are achieved together. Virtue is not a zero-sum game.

Wisdom

The virtue of wisdom is twofold. First, it is prudence, which guides our actions. Prudence is a knack for distinguishing ends and means. It allows us to see what we should do in a given situation. Without it, we lack insight and direction. Second, it is wisdom proper, which is attentive to the nature of things, especially the true, the good, and the beautiful. Heraclitus says, "Thinking well is the greatest excellence and wisdom: to act and speak what is true, perceiving things according to their nature."[15] These natures are not subject to our choice; we cannot change what they are. But we can contemplate and appreciate them wherever they appear. When we do so, we gain the perspective necessary for acting ethically and realizing what it means to be free. Bertrand Russell puts it as follows:

> The impartiality which, in contemplation, is the unalloyed desire for truth, is the very same quality of mind which, in action, is justice, and in emotion is that universal love

14. Safer, "Flavorists."
15. Heraclitus, *Art and Thought of Heraclitus*, 43.

which can be given to all, and not only to those who are judged useful or admirable. Thus contemplation enlarges not only the objects of our thoughts, but also the objects of our actions and our affections: it makes us citizens of the universe, not only of one walled city at war with all the rest. In this citizenship of the universe consists man's true freedom, and his liberation from the thralldom of narrow hopes and fears.[16]

Wisdom is the kind of knowledge about those things that are highest and best, and it makes true freedom possible. I will have more to say about wisdom and freedom in subsequent chapters.

With moderation, courage, justice, and wisdom, we can enjoy a divine existence, but without them a merely bestial one. As Aristotle observes, "For man, when perfected, is the best of animals, but, when separated from law and justice, he is the worst of all, since armed injustice is the more dangerous, and he is equipped at birth with arms, meant to be used by intelligence and excellence, which he may use for the worst ends. Wherefore, if he have not virtue, he is the most unholy and the most savage of animals, and the most full of lust and gluttony."[17] Virtues and institutions humanize our animal desires, making them properly interpersonal.

Why Be Good?

Plato asks us to imagine a magical ring called the Ring of Gyges, which makes its wearer disappear.[18] If we could do anything we want without getting caught, wouldn't we all do everything we could to get ahead, including theft and voyeurism? Would guaranteed anonymity lead us to vicious behavior? In other words, are we only good because we fear the consequences of having a bad reputation? Plato responds that virtue is its own reward and we should seek it no matter what. Only virtuous people make good

16. Russell, *Problems of Philosophy*, 161.
17. Aristotle, *Politics* 1.2, 1253a31–39.
18. Plato, *Republic* 359c–360d.

friends, and only virtuous people are good friends to themselves. If we are not virtuous but mediocre, we are only capable of mediocre relationships. We might be able to enjoy some activity with another, or we might help in time of need, but we are not able to delight in our goodness or that of our friends.

The film *Gladiator* portrayed this powerfully. Marcus Aurelius, the philosopher-king, decides that his son cannot succeed him to the throne because he is not a moral man. When informed of the decision, the son, Commodos, points out that while he doesn't have any of the cardinal virtues, he is ambitious and devoted. Wickedly, he suffocates his father in order to claim the crown for himself, while moaning that he only ever wanted to be loved. Though he wants to be loved, he does not want to become lovable. He successfully becomes king and quickly becomes consumed by jealousy, lust, and anger. He is never successful at provoking anyone to love him.

Absent virtue, our friendships can only be based on pleasure or utility, not on mutual goodness. There is a difference between enjoying a TV show with a friend or even enjoying talking to a friend and enjoying the very existence of that friend. Aristotle imagines what a person would be like without the cardinal virtues of courage, moderation, justice, or wisdom:

> No one would maintain that he is happy who has not in him a particle of courage or moderation or justice or wisdom, who is afraid of every insect which flutters past him, and who will commit any crime, however great, in order to gratify his lust of meat or drink, who will sacrifice his dearest friend for the sake of several dollars, and is as feeble and false in mind as a child or a madman.[19]

Who would want to be such a person, and who would want to be his or her friend? To be good, we need to be courageous, moderate, just, and wise. We need the virtues to be successful at being human both for ourselves and for others. The better we are, the more we are capable of love. Virtuous humans are also beauties to behold,

19. Aristotle, *Politics* 7.1, 1323a27–34; translation modified.

44

which is why Socrates, famously ugly, was nonetheless irresistibly attractive. Virtue has its own kind of allure.

Happiness:
Subjective Satisfaction in an Objective Form

Aristotle says that the mark of virtuous people is not only that they do what it right but that they delight in doing it. The person who begrudgingly or with great struggle does what is right is a decent person, but he or she has not attained virtue, and so he or she has not obtained that inner freedom from constraint characteristic of virtue. For the virtuous person has internalized the good and no longer experiences it as a foreign obligation. Understanding and delighting in it, no matter how difficult, the virtuous person not only does good but *is good*. The activity and presence of such a person is itself a delight, and so virtuous people make the very best of friends. Of course, the ideal of virtue is difficult to achieve, but to the degree to which we do achieve it, to that degree we achieve human flourishing, and to that degree we are capable of the very best of friendships. Our freedom, then, can clothe us in virtues, allowing us to don a second nature truly in keeping with the high calling of the human person. Human happiness has an objective form specified by our human nature, but it requires human freedom to be realized, and its realization brings with it joy. Just as a child plays without strain, so the virtuous individual is good and does what is good without strain, and thus with a great degree of pleasure.

The conventional idea equates happiness and pleasure; it regards happiness as merely subjective satisfaction. By contrast, the philosophical view says that happiness is the greatest human achievement; it regards happiness as having an objective form and a subjective satisfaction. A person who subjectively feels good in a virtual world while he fails in the real one is not objectively flourishing. He is not truly happy. He might feel good, but he is not realizing his inborn potential. Like the wilting plant, his life is not a beauty to behold. Because his nature is unfulfilled, even his feeling of pleasure will not be complete. It will leave him empty and unsatisfied. The subjective notion of happiness will not objectively satisfy us.

Aristotle recommends we repeat to ourselves concerning pleasure what the elders of Troy said of Helen: "Terrible is the likeness of her face to immortal goddesses. Still, though she be such, let her go away in the ships, lest she be left behind, a grief to us and our children."[20] Pleasure is a terrible good that can easily lead to our ruin. While virtue has its own pleasure, pursuing pleasure generally comes at the expense of virtue. Seek virtue, and you get pleasure as a kind of bonus; seek pleasure, and you forsake virtue and quite often pleasure too.

If it *feels* good, should we do it? Only if it *is* good. By doing what is good, we'll become good. And, when we are good, doing good will even feel good.

20. Homer, *Iliad*, 3, lines 158–60.

5

Is Life about Creating Yourself?

[Freedom]

According to the U.S. Supreme Court, we are free to create meaning for ourselves: "At the heart of liberty is the right to define one's own concept of existence, of meaning, of the universe, and of the mystery of human life."[1] (Apparently, liberty does not include the right to define one's own concept of liberty; we just have to accept the one chosen for us by the Court.) The quotation summarizes, perfectly, freedom's conventional understanding. Freedom allows each of us to impose meaning upon the chaos of our lives. In an even more quotable form (I've even seen it on a T-shirt), we read: "Life isn't about finding yourself. Life is about creating yourself." The quotation is sometimes attributed to the playwright George Bernard Shaw.

Let's take a look at this bit of wisdom. It consists of a negation followed by an affirmation. What does it deny? "Life isn't about finding oneself." No amount of seeking or thinking will enable us to happen upon ourselves, to discover some intrinsic meaning, to find ourselves. So this is what it denies. What does it affirm? "Life is about creating oneself." This cannot mean that we bring ourselves into being in the way that God creates the world, for we

---

1. United States Supreme Court, *Planned Parenthood of Southeastern Pennsylvania v. Casey.*

47

would have to exist before we existed, which is impossible. Rather this is a bit more like when a chef says of a dish, "This is my greatest creation." We are dough in our own hands. The meaning of our human existence is not set but is for us to decide and make.

Here's the rub: on what basis can we decide what to create? Aren't we *forced* to decide *arbitrarily* what life means? And, if so, is this really freedom or rather a curse? To illustrate this difficulty, we can consider an example from medieval philosophy, called "Buridan's Ass." Imagine a donkey placed midway between two identical bales of hay. It would starve to death, because it would have no reason to move one way rather than another. Now imagine that the bales of hay are removed and we are that donkey. How are we to decide which way to go, what life means? There is nothing for us to find or discover; we must simply choose. Unless we can find some reason for preferring one way to another, we just have to be random.

But this freedom to decide arbitrarily what life means is not the same kind of freedom we experience in other aspects of our lives. The fact is that whenever an artist creates something, she already has in mind some idea of what is good and beautiful. She doesn't decide these first but learns them. For instance, the chef knows her spices and knows what they can do, and she knows what a good dish tastes like. She does not create the spices, and she does not create the standards of taste; instead she creates the dish that uses known spices to meet those standards. A great artist, it is true, will not just meet known standards, but will reveal new ones. Apple's Steve Jobs, for instance, didn't use focus groups, because he wanted to give people things they had never even thought to desire.[2] Jobs was not arbitrary—he had a keen sense for what people would want and that is what he gave them. Like creativity, freedom is not arbitrary but is rooted in the perception of the good and the beautiful. Descartes accordingly thinks freedom is the ability to achieve the good: "In order to be free, there is no need for me to be inclined both ways; on the contrary, the more I incline in

---

2. Kahney, "Ten Commandments of Steve," 35.

one direction—either because I clearly understand that reasons of truth and goodness point that way, or because of a divinely produced disposition of my inmost thoughts—the freer is my choice."[3]

Know Thyself

The ancient Greeks had their own mottos, though they did not, as far as I know, write them on their togas. One of the most important of these was chiseled above the door of the oracle at Delphi. It is the command: "Know Thyself." Rather than *Don't bother knowing thyself, but create thyself,* they declared *Know thyself.* For the philosopher, "Know thyself" became a command to authenticity, the route to the best way of life. Heraclitus says, "I went in search of myself,"[4] and Socrates says:

> I have no time for [petty concerns]; and the reason, my friend, is this. I am still unable, as the Delphic inscription orders, to know myself; and it really seems to me ridiculous to look into other things before I have understood that . . . I look not into them but into my own self.[5]

Philosophers want to know whether they are virtuous or full of vice. They ask, *What kind of person am I?* Good, bad, or mediocre? If we are honest with ourselves, there is yet the possibility of becoming what we should like to be.

Whenever we do something, whether it's pitching, playing the piano, being a doctor, being a friend, or being a mother, it is not enough simply to do these things. It is more satisfying to be a good doctor than a bad one, and as a patient I'd much rather go to a good doctor than a bad one. It is not enough simply to be a friend; the only kind worth being and worth having is a good one. Similarly, it is not enough simply to be a mother or a father; that much is easily done; instead we want to be good mothers and good fathers and there is no end of sorrow if you are the child of bad

3. Descartes, *Meditations on First Philosophy*, 40.

4. Heraclitus, *Art and Thought of Heraclitus*, 41.

5. Plato, *Phaedrus* 230a; translation modified.

parents. If every one of our important activities is like this, might it not be the case that the whole of our lives is like this? Is it enough simply to be a human being? For that much is easily done. Or, as in pitching, parenting, and playing, do we want to be good at what we do and who we are? And, if we are to be good at what we do and who we are, aren't we going to have to practice in earnest?

Free to Become Good

Ancient thinkers sought to know human nature, but in our own day we deny there is a nature to be known. How did we arrive at this state of affairs? In the Renaissance, Giovanni Pico della Miran-dola retold the creation account with a new twist. Rather than give human beings a nature, as in the Genesis account, Pico says that the human being is the one being lacking a nature. Why is that? According to his telling of the tale, God created all other creatures first, from earthworms to angels, giving them fixed natures, but when God came to human beings, he had no natures left to give them. What did God do instead? He gave human beings *freedom*. Here we have the origin of the contemporary opposition of nature and freedom. In Pico, however, our freedom still has direction. God gives human beings freedom so that they can choose their own natures; that is, they can choose to live like the beasts or they can strive to acquire an angelic or even divine nature.[6] Pico thinks the obvious choice is the latter, but his suggestion that nature and freedom are opposed and that human freedom is a kind of alien force unlike anything else under the sun came to dominate how people think about themselves. Closer to our own time, Jean-Paul Sartre perfectly expresses the cultural view by saying we are "condemned to be free."[7] We find ourselves existing and have to choose for ourselves what we are going to be: "Man is nothing else but what he makes of himself."[8] Can this be right? Is freedom arbitrary?

6. Pico, "Oration on the Dignity of Man," 5–11.
7. Sartre, "Existentialism," 23.
8. Ibid., 15.

John Locke distinguishes between *liberty* and what he calls *license*. Liberty is the ability to achieve good, and it requires reason and the ability to know the true good, to be able to recognize what he calls the natural law, something to which everyone is subject. Whether you are Polish or Peruvian, an American or an Argentinian, you are bound by the natural law to be just to yourself and others. License, by contrast, is simply the ability to do whatever you want whenever you want. Locke says that children are not capable of liberty but only of license, and anybody who has ever had children in their care immediately knows what he means: if you give children everything they want, say all the candy or toys they can lay their hands on, they will have a meltdown, becoming something dangerous to themselves and others. They quickly become deeply troubled and soon become spoiled brats. Because they don't know what is really good, children are not really free. They have whim but not liberty, because true freedom requires knowledge of the good. That's why parents have authority over children: to enable their children to learn the truth about being human so that the child will mature to liberty. For Locke, when we act unjustly, we are not really acting freely. We have license, but not liberty.

Locke's way of thinking is foreign to conventional wisdom, so another example might be helpful. Adding is a kind of mathematical operation that puts two numbers together to get a third. However, when someone adds 2 and 2 and gets 5, they haven't really added. Adding is not just putting numbers together; it's putting numbers together *correctly*. Similarly, when I fail to achieve the good, I haven't really fulfilled the meaning of freedom. Without knowledge of the good, we might make choices, but those choices will be arbitrary, and they won't achieve what we want them to: happiness and human flourishing. Liberty isn't just choosing; it's choosing the good.

Pico and our conventional wisdom are committed to a false dilemma in which we have to choose between a fixed nature that makes us unfree and no nature that makes freedom arbitrary. But we can follow Aristotle and say the following: our human nature gives us certain inclinations towards the good that we can freely develop so that they become second nature.[9] Every human being has the desire and the ability to develop the virtues. So, if someone trains to be good, he or she can become good, and such an achievement fulfills the natural capacity and trajectory proper to his or her human nature. For Aristotle, then, human nature is not static but is a dynamic propensity for development. John Stuart Mill similarly says, "Human nature is not a machine to be built after a model, and set to do exactly the work prescribed for it, but a tree, which requires to grow and develop itself on all sides, according to the tendency of the inward forces which make it a living thing."[10] Freedom is not constrained but liberated by the stirrings inscribed into human nature. I do not have to create virtue and then become virtuous; virtue is already a natural possibility waiting to be freely realized. Freedom and nature are not opposed. On the contrary, without nature, freedom would be a curse, and without some degree of freedom, nature would be lifeless.

An objection to this account goes as follows: what if someone freely develops vice? Surely that is a possibility inborn in nature too? And if so, how are we to decide between virtue and vice, two trajectories of our nature? Isn't it again *arbitrary*? But the difference between a good baseball player and a bad one is not arbitrary, even though both are genuine possibilities for baseball. A virtuous person fulfills human nature in a way that a vicious person does not. If we want to be like a virtuous person, it is the virtue itself we find attractive; if we want to be like a vicious person, it is something they possess that we find attractive. When we emulate bad role models, we want the money, power, or pleasure they have; if they did not have such things, we wouldn't find them attractive. By contrast, we emulate good role models even when they don't have money, power, and pleasure. We don't want something they *have*; we want *to be the kind of person they are*. Virtue resonates with our own nature.

9. Aristotle, *Nicomachean Ethics* 2.1.
10. Mill, *On Liberty*, 72.

Free to Be Human

At the heart of liberty is the overwhelming desire to seek the truth concerning existence, meaning, the universe, and the mystery of human life and to develop ourselves accordingly. Arbitrariness constrains rather than liberates, but truth truly sets us free. Freedom, then, is involved in our development, but it is not the absolute freedom suggested by the command: "Create thyself." We do not create ourselves, but finding ourselves with a particular nature destined for happiness, we have the responsibility to cultivate those virtues that will fulfill our natures and thereby make us happy. Life is about striving so that goodness becomes second nature. We are free, then, to become fully human.

6

Are We Supposed to Be Selfless?

[Love]

After I gave a conference paper on love in Plato and Augustine, a graduate student in sociology came up to me and asked, "How can you believe in love?" In her eyes was a look of desperation. It was clear she wanted to believe in love but could not bring herself to do so. Why not? The social sciences testify to a suspicion alive in the contemporary mind. Love is supposed to be selfless, but no human act is ever selfless. People always get some kind of satisfaction or benefit from acts of supposed love. Therefore, love seems to be impossible.

Philosophers approach the question of love from a different angle. Nietzsche, for one, argues that selfless love, far from being the highest good, amounts to a denial of the goodness of life. We are told to prize the self of another over and instead of our own self only because it is, well, *other* than our own. We are supposed to love others simply because they are not us. Scheler puts the problem with this view as follows: "If I myself am not worthy of love, why should the 'other' be? As if he were not also an 'I'—for himself and I 'another'—for him!"[1] Everyone around me is supposed to love me selflessly. But if love is selfless, then I can't love myself in this way. Absurdly, then, no one loves himself, but everybody else

1. Scheler, *Ressentiment*, 87.

is supposed to. Is each of us lovable or not? The ideal of selfless love makes no sense.

Love Flows Back

But doesn't one of the greatest teachers of all time tell us to love selflessly? Jesus says, "Deny yourself." But he also says, "Love your neighbor *as yourself.*" He takes self-love to be the measure and standard of loving another. Kierkegaard puts it this way: "To love yourself in the right way and to love the neighbor correspond perfectly to one another; fundamentally they are one and the same thing."[2] Aristotle says something similar. In order to love another we have to love ourselves and regard the beloved as another self. Here love is not self*less*, not a denial of one's self. Rather it is a fundamental expansion of one's self, an affirmation of the goodness of one's self, including one's power to love as well as the goodness of the person one loves.

No less a Christian thinker than Saint Thomas Aquinas says that only God is the maximally liberal giver, who gives without gain. Every creature, by contrast, gains in giving, and there is nothing wrong with that; it is rather a reminder that we are on our way and have a lot of growing to do.[3] This does not mean that we do everything with an ulterior motive and should always seek our own private advantage. Rather it means that acts of love benefit both the beloved *and* the lover. Yes, love involves sacrifice. A mother and father must sacrifice many things for the sake of their children. But this is not to act selflessly. For one of the greatest glories of being a person is being a great mother and father and having the company of children who have turned out well. This is among the most personally satisfying things the human being is capable of. So the parents have in fact sacrificed their desires to develop a hobby or to advance in their career or to read books or make art so that they can achieve a still higher good: bringing forth into the

2. Kierkegaard, *Works of Love*, 22.
3. *Summa Theologiae*, I, q. 44, a. 4, ad 1.

world children capable of love, who appreciate the true, the good, and the beautiful, and who are therefore enjoyable to be around. Helping people is bilateral; the person helped is not exclusively in our debt. The sacrifices of love are as much for the beloved as for the lover, who chooses the value of love over everything else and thereby proves his or her worth as a lover. When we give a beggar change, we gain more than he does insofar as we gain a spiritual good, generosity, and he something merely material, food.

Now, just because love benefits the self does not mean we may make that benefit our motive. We shouldn't. If I do an act of love for my own benefit, then it is not an act of love. It has to be for the advantage of the beloved. Let's say a husband buys flowers for his wife, knowing full well that they will put her in a good mood. Now, it is beneficial to him to have his wife be in good spirits. But this can't be his motive; his concern, provided that he loves his wife, should be for her well-being. However, in love, the good of the beloved is the good of the lover. Consequently, he should not deny his interest in his wife's well-being. In caring for her, he likewise becomes a good husband. In love, our self and another become entwined, so that sorting out benefits becomes absurd. Do good for loved ones and gratefully receive the good that comes from doing so. Just don't make that the end. Care with wild abandon for the other and you will gain your true self. That's not selfless love. That's love that enlarges life.

Neither Selfless nor Selfish

Am I missing something? Isn't there something true about love's selflessness insofar as love is opposed to being selfish? Yes, love is not selfish. People who are greedy, lustful, cowardly, and otherwise devoid of virtue can't love, because they seek a good for themselves at the expense of others. However, the good they pursue for themselves is a sham. They want money whatever the costs, they want pleasure no matter what, they want to protect themselves instead of others. They don't really benefit themselves. So they get money but no one to enjoy it with, they get pleasure but without the satisfaction of meaning, or they dishonorably fail to protect those entrusted to their care. Selfish people don't do good for themselves. However, to love is to will the good of the beloved. So the selfish person doesn't really love himself or herself, as Kierkegaard points out: "When the bustler wastes his time and powers in the service of futile, inconsequential pursuits, is this not because he has not learned rightly to love himself? When the light-minded person throws himself almost like a nonentity into the folly of the moment and makes nothing of it, is this not because he does not know how to love himself rightly?"[4] So, love is not a matter of selfishly pitting oneself against others. It is a matter of recognizing the community of self and other founded in a good common to each. In love, we seek the common good and all of us benefit. Similarly, Jesus teaches us to die to ourselves in order to come into our own; just as a seed must cease to be a seed in order to become a plant, so we must let go of egoism in the name of love in order to be fully ourselves.

There is a possibility of pride in which people pursue virtue for self-glorification and not for the sake of love. Here honor and being honored is placed above being good. In Jane Austen's *Pride and Prejudice*, the lead protagonist, Fitzwilliam Darcy, is brought through love to the recognition that his virtue had been distorted by pride. In the scene where he and his beloved, Elizabeth Bennet, can finally profess their love openly, he says:

> I have been a selfish being all my life, in practice, though not in principle. As a child I was taught what was right, but I was not taught to correct my temper. I was given good principles, but left to follow them in pride and conceit. Unfortunately an only son (for many years an only child), I was spoilt by my parents, who, though good themselves (my father, particularly, all that was benevolent and amiable), allowed, encouraged, almost taught me to be selfish and overbearing; to care for none beyond my own family circle; to think meanly of all the rest of the

4. Kierkegaard, *Works of Love*, 23.

world; to wish at least to think meanly of their sense and worth compared with my own. Such I was, from eight to eight and twenty; and such I might still have been but for you, dearest, loveliest Elizabeth! What do I not owe you! You taught me a lesson, hard indeed at first, but most advantageous. By you, I was properly humbled.[5]

He is humbled because he discovers that he was unlovable and that his supposed virtue was a sham. Yet his love for Elizabeth led him to want to become lovable, to want to act out of love instead of vanity. And he does indeed become lovable through repeated acts of love. As Austen shows, the antidote to selfishness is not selflessness but love: "What do I not owe you!" In love, we gain rather than lose ourselves.

Is It Better to Love or Be Loved?

People want to think of themselves as lovable. Hence they desire to be loved, for actuality proves potentiality (if they *are* loved, they must be lovable).[6] Yet they find that being loved does not make one lovable. It is not enough to be loved. We only want to be loved by those who know us intimately, because only those in the know are in a position to judge whether we are in fact lovable. The celebrity soon discovers the adoration of fans is not enough. The politician soon discovers that the love of the masses does not satisfy. It's not the quantity of friends but the quality of friends that we want, for we want someone to come into our depths with us. For we suspect if we were really known, we would not be loved. We cannot help but wonder, why should anyone ever love *me*?

What we miss here is a point grasped by many a philosopher. The ability to love makes one loveable (and spellbindingly beautiful). Actualizing that possibility proves the potentiality. (If we *do*

5. Austen, *Pride and Prejudice*, ch. 58.

6. In a different context, Aristotle remarks, "What convinces is the possible; now whereas we are not yet sure as to the possibility of that which has not happened, that which has happened is manifestly possible, otherwise it would not have happened" (*Poetics* 9, 1451b17–18).

love, then clearly we *can* love.) Even the ugly Socrates appeared unspeakably beautiful to those around him due to the quality of his love. Now, the sort of love philosophers have in mind is nothing superficial. As Wittgenstein observes, "Love is not a feeling. Love is put to the test, pain not. One does not say: 'That was not true pain, or it would not have gone off so quickly.'"[7] But of course we do say, "That was not true love." Why? Because unlike a feeling, which comes and goes, love is an act of the will, a deed, that puts into play the entire resources of a person. If someone proves unfaithful, that person proves he didn't really love. How one loves is a measure of the kind of person one is. Love is primarily loving rather than being loved, for it is in loving that we prove we are lovable. In fact, in sole justification of the priority of loving over being loved, Aristotle points to mothers who for the good of their children give them up for adoption even though this means never being loved by them in return.[8] These mothers are supremely lovable, because they truly are capable of the greatest love.

Sacrificial Love

A father holds his baby in his arms ready at any moment to lay down his life for hers. Isn't this selfless love? He wants to protect his daughter at all costs even up to and including the sacrifice of his own life, because he holds her to be an absolute good entrusted to his fatherly care. It would be his greatest glory as a father to make such a sacrifice; to fail to make that sacrifice when necessary would be the greatest dishonor. It is not, then, an issue of disregarding himself but of knowing his high calling as father to this child. Such love involves self-love, but the focus is on the love of the other. Why teach? The students gain, but so does the teacher. Teaching is the highest mode of learning, and the teacher has the satisfaction of seeing her beloved students grow. Give and don't

---

7. Wittgenstein, *Zettel*, §504.
8. Aristotle, *Nicomachean Ethics* 8.8.

[Love]

count the costs, but don't give because it costs. Give because there is a love for the recipient and glory in the giving.

7

Is Death Important (or Can We Ignore It)?

[Life]

Zombies grip the American psyche. But even though the walking dead populate our movies and our imagination, they do not make us confront what the ancient Greeks referred to as the Necessity: each of us, whether we would like to or not, must die. We moderns do not refer to *our* eventual death at all. It doesn't come up in our conversation. Perhaps our fascination with zombies is an attempt to run from death and to regard it as something that happens to other people—and not to us. When death does obtrude, in the form of a funeral motorcade or the wakeless sleep of a public figure, we find it inconvenient, but we pay our respects. When death strikes closer to home, robbing us of a loved one, then we pay attention, at least for a while. But we cannot bear the thought of death, so our attention soon turns to things we can. We hardly ever face the fact that each of us will surely die.

Pascal thinks that we do the things we do to run from our mortality. "Being unable to cure death, wretchedness and ignorance, men have decided, in order to be happy, not to think about such things."[1] He sees the failure to confront death as a principal cause of human mischief. "Sometimes, when I set to thinking

1. Pascal, *Pensées*, 37.

about the various activities of men, the dangers and troubles which they face at Court, or in war, giving rise to so many quarrels and passions, daring and often wicked enterprises and so on, I have often said that *the sole cause of man's unhappiness is that he does not know how to stay quietly in his room.*[2] Since death is so vexing a possibility and since we find ourselves powerless before it, we run and bury our head in the sand of this, that, or the other distraction. We can't cure death, so we go shopping.

Plato thinks death sheds light on life. He calls philosophy the art of dying well: "the one aim of those who practice philosophy in the proper manner is to practice for dying and death."[3] Only when we are sick do we realize, by its painful absence, how wonderful it is to be healthy. Confronting sickness, then, makes health appear more profoundly. Similarly, confronting death makes life appear more profoundly. Death reminds us what life is supposed to be about. In contrast to conventional wisdom, then, philosophers want us to face our mortality. But don't people who dwell on death become morbid, dreary, and pessimistic? On the contrary, there's no need to be a bore. Being mindful of death is something else altogether.

We Mortals

The ancient Greeks called us humans "mortals," because we are the ones that confront our mortality. The term underscores the fact that we are not masters of our lives. Instead, we find ourselves vulnerable to suffering and death. Such mortality reveals our finitude, the fact that we are limited and bounded. We are finite not only because death awaits us in the future; we are finite because at any given moment, in any given day, there is only so much that can be done. The limit of our lives and the limit of our days means that our choices matter. We have no time to waste.

2. Ibid. (italics added).
3. Plato, *Phaedo* 64a.

Philosophers have exerted more effort thinking about death (the end) rather than birth (the beginning), but birth is even more important.[4] For death is what it is, an existential threat to each one of us, only because each one of us already exists. Without anyone having consulted us, we came to be here in the world, and only because we have come to be can we potentially lose that being in death. We can conceive a birth without a corresponding death, but there could be no death if there were not first a birth. Our lives are bounded by birth and death, natality and mortality, an absent past and an absent future, each day beginning and ending. We cannot master these limits, but these limits grant us the time to be and master the things we can. How is it that we are able to reach beyond the present to comprehend ourselves as temporally limited?

Language allows us to transcend the immediacy of the present. It allows us to wonder about our future and our past. It allows us to have a sense of self persisting through time, to say "I" of ourselves and address others as "you." It allows us to be responsible for others and to give thanks for the things we have. Language enables us to wonder about the death that awaits each of us in the unknown future. Without language, we would be wed to the present and our biologically relevant environments. We are the mortals we are because we have language. While Darwin thinks we're not much different than other animals, he admits that humans are the only living beings to think about death: "It may be freely admitted that no animal is self-conscious, if by this term it is implied, that he reflects on such points, as whence he comes or whither he will go, or what is life and death, and so forth."[5] Or as Heidegger succinctly puts it, "Only man dies. The animal perishes."[6]

We have all heard someone exclaim in anguish, "I am so embarrassed I could just die." Our mortal selves are especially manifest in shame, when we are vulnerable to the uncharitable gaze of others. Why do we care what people think of us? What difference

4. Arendt thinks the importance of birth emerges for the first time in the thought of Augustine. See Arendt, *Life of the Mind*, 2:109.

5. Darwin, *Descent of Man*, 297.

6. Heidegger, "Thing," 178.

does it make? And even if we don't do something wrong or silly, why don't we want people prying into our personal affairs or staring at us? Clearly, human beings have a personal dignity that longs for the respect—rather than derision—of others. Darwin, in fact, regards blushing as the most distinctively human emotion.[7]

Each of us is vulnerable to shame, and this vulnerability entails a twofold responsibility. First, we should not do anything shameful. For instance, once in Rome I unwittingly played the role of the ugly American by walking down the street while eating a slice of pizza. Romans stared at my behavior in disbelief, and I keenly felt their displeasure at the spectacle. Only later did I come to realize that food is not fuel and one should never eat in front of others who are not eating, especially since some might go hungry. The second responsibility entailed by shame is to respect others. Gossips and tabloids want to put everything, whether good or bad, out there for public comment and possible ridicule. Respect, however, holds that the dignity of each person and the details of their lives should not be exposed to unnecessary exposition and scorn. While character matters for our politicians, our leaders, and our own friends, the private details of everybody else's lives are none of our business. With respect, then, we care about ourselves enough not to do shameful things, and we care about others enough not to expose them to needless ridicule. Friendship and love allow us to reveal ourselves without fear of danger. Our vulnerability, then, enables the intimacy of friends and loved ones.

There are further ethical implications to our mortality. In nature, animals starve and other animals eat them. That's just the way it is. But when it comes to the human being, we have a choice, and the ruthless natural law of eat or be eaten is suspended. It would be silly to try to stop seals from being eaten by polar bears (what would polar bears eat?), but we have a responsibility to do what we can to keep humans from being eaten. The Jewish philosopher Emmanuel Lévinas devoted himself to this insight. During World War II, most of his family was killed in concentration camps, and

---

7. Darwin, *Expression of Emotions in Man and Animals*, 310.

he spent time in a Russian prisoner-of-war camp. The Russians treated the prisoners cruelly, and he marveled that only Bobby, a dog that wandered onto the camp, seemed aware that the prisoners were human beings. Lévinas argues that when we allow ourselves to encounter other mortal selves, we experience their vulnerability and our corresponding responsibility for them. Now we might think such responsibility is burdensome, but Lévinas assures us that, on the contrary, responsibility enhances our lives by inspiring us to become good: "Thus in expression the being that imposes itself does not limit but promotes my freedom, by arousing my goodness."[8] Lévinas's guards evaded their responsibility, but in doing so they undermined their liberty. Each of us has a special responsibility to other human beings because of the kind of beings they are: other mortal selves.

What Is to Become of Us?

What happens at death? Do we simply cease to be, returning to nothingness (annihilation)? Or does some part of us continue to exist (immortality)? Among philosophers, Hume notably championed annihilation and Socrates immortality, and we know that both bravely faced their own deaths. A friend visited Hume on his deathbed. He was shocked at how peaceful Hume was just before sliding into the oblivion of nonbeing:

> I asked him if it was not possible that there might be a future state. He answered It was possible that a piece of coal put upon the fire would not burn; and he added that it was a most unreasonable fancy that we should exist for ever. That immortality, if it were at all, must be general; that a great proportion of the human race has hardly any intellectual qualities; that a great proportion dies in infancy before being possessed of reason; yet all these must be immortal; that a Porter who gets drunk by ten o'clock with gin must be immortal; that the trash of every age

8. Lévinas, *Totality and Infinity*, 200.

must be preserved, and that new Universes must be created to contain such infinite numbers.[9]

In the face of annihilation, Hume remained serene and self-confi-
dent: "I asked him if the thought of Annihilation never gave him
any uneasiness. He said not the least; no more than the thought
that he had not been, as Lucretius observes."[10]

We find Socrates similarly full of good cheer just before his
death. He tells his puzzled companions why he is full of hope:

> For, Simmias and Cebes, I should be wrong not to resent
> dying if I did not believe that I should go first to other
> wise and good gods, and then to men who have died
> and are better than men are here. Be assured that, as it
> is, I expect to join the company of good men. This last I
> would not altogether insist on, but if I insist on anything
> at all in these matters, it is that I shall come to gods who
> are very good masters. That is why I am not so resentful,
> because I have good hope that some future awaits men
> after death, as we have been told for years, a much better
> future for the good than for the wicked.[11]

Socrates has good reason to believe and hope that his life will be
rewarded with a happy afterlife. Who's right: Hume or Socrates?
What can we hope awaits us on the other side of death? Oblivion
or a future life?

When I sit next to someone and look into her eyes or view her
actions, her very life is quite palpable. But then we see her die, and
her flesh turns pale, her motions cease, and what she was no longer
presents itself to me. Physiologically, all that wonderful aliveness
of metabolizing, neural happening, and blood pumping stops, and
the bodily structure begins to break down, resolving itself into
more stable, simpler elements. Can I infer from this absence of the
other person to her not existing at all?

---

9. Boswell, "Account of My Last Interview with David Hume, Esq.," 76–77.
10. Ibid., 77.
11. Plato, *Phaedo* 63b–c.

Let's turn it around: When I sit next to someone and she looks into my eyes or views my actions, my very life is quite palpable to her. But when she sees me die, my flesh turns pale, my motions cease, and what I was no longer presents itself to her. Can she infer from my absence to my nonexistence? Only if my presence can be identified with the physiological happening. Only, that is, if science can know everything there is to know about me.

On the biological level, we are a complex machine consisting of basically chemical processes. On the physical level, we are clouds of particles in fields of force. When the biological machine breaks down altering our fundamental physics, then it seems we simply cease to be. The great scientist Stephen Hawking thinks in this way: "I regard the brain as a computer which will stop working when its components fail. There is no heaven or afterlife for broken down computers; that is a fairy story for people afraid of the dark."[12]

Can anything be said, philosophically, on behalf of this "fairy story"? Plato points to the experience of truth, beauty, and goodness to argue that there is more to us than biological processes. Now, one scientist writes: "Living organisms had existed on earth, without ever knowing why, for over three thousand million years before the truth finally dawned on one of them. His name was Charles Darwin."[13] The truth of evolution occurred to Darwin, however, not because he was an organism, but because he was the kind of thing that could know truth. No centipede, dolphin, chimpanzee, or dog could have discovered evolution, because these species are geared to their specific environments. Only the human being stands above the surrounding world to contemplate the grand scheme of things. Similarly, at the beach, the sublime experience of beauty awes us. The scene swarms with organisms: seagulls circling overhead, sea lions frolicking in the foam, seaweed washing in on the sand. We humans, however, are the only ones to whom this spectacular display stands open in its awe-inspiring

---

12. Sample, "Stephen Hawking: 'There is no heaven; it's a fairy story.'"
13. Dawkins, *Selfish Gene*, 1.

beauty. We can be struck by the beauty of nature, an experience that is true and yet biologically irrelevant. Also, we are responsible for the good. We can understand and follow the Golden Rule, even when it would be to the advantage of our kin to do otherwise. Therefore, we give money to the poor and not just to our own children. The good is biologically irrelevant. The true, the beautiful, and the good, then, indicate a dimension in us that exceeds the merely biological. The human ability to live in this dimension and thereby to love another and oneself is a fundamental fact of our nature. Human dignity and our fundamental moral responsibility for each other flow from this personal dimension.

Søren Kierkegaard thinks that the best proof for immortality came from Socrates's courageous hope in immortality, a hope that shaped the very way he lived his life. To be able to live for immortality shows a dimension in us that outstrips the biological. In this way, Socrates does not prove immortality through logic but through life. Objectively, he asks *if* there is an immortality. Subjectively, he dedicates his whole life to its reality: "On this 'if' he risks his entire life, he has the courage to meet death, and he has with the passion of the infinite so determined the pattern of his life that it must be found acceptable—*if* there is an immortality. Is any better proof capable of being given for the immortality of the soul?"[14] In this way, Hume's courage before his annihilation would in fact prove the opposite position, namely, that there is a personal freedom that defies the merely biological.

The argument for death as annihilation goes as follows: we are nothing but complex biological systems; at death the complex material structures resolve into simpler elements; therefore, at death, we cease to be. The argument for personal immortality goes as follows: the personal dimension of our existence, the bearer of dignity (what it is to be me, to know truth, to contemplate beauty, to be responsible for the good, and so forth) cannot be explained in terms of matter alone; death affects the matter alone; therefore, at death, the person can survive. On the one hand, the annihilation

14. Kierkegaard, *Concluding Unscientific Postscript*, 180.

position seems to underplay our human appetite for truth and corresponding dignity. We appear as just another kind of organism rather than as persons. On the other, the immortality crowd seems to underplay the importance of our bodies. Socrates even refers to our bodies as prisons we do well to leave. Accordingly, some philosophers try to find an alternative.

Immanuel Kant thinks both positions are in philosophical hot water. Both assume we know exactly what we are, but in fact we only know how we appear. The annihilists cannot prove that we are only a biological machine, and the immortalists cannot prove that there is something that is not biological in us. We can prove neither that death means annihilation nor that we survive.[15] Kant thinks the existence of an afterlife is a certain belief, because otherwise our hope for happiness and moral perfection would be groundless.[16] In questioning the demonstrations of both sides, Kant tries to make room for a rational faith in an afterlife.

Another attempt to reconcile these two camps comes from Thomas Aquinas, who argues that while part of us does survive death, we are essentially incomplete without our bodies. He mounts a philosophical defense of immortality in view of our appetite for truth and our desire for continued existence: evidently, we transcend the merely biological.[17] He also defends the importance of our bodies in view of the role of the senses in coming to know truth: without our senses we couldn't learn anything, and without our brains we couldn't remember anything.[18] Aquinas thinks both the immortality of our souls and the need for our bodies can be reconciled in terms of the specifically religious belief in the resurrection of the body. Then, our immortal souls would be united with transformed mortal bodies, and we would be complete once again. It was in following this line of reasoning that Wittgenstein, who kept religion at arm's length, nonetheless felt the allure of Christianity:

15. Kant, *Prolegomena*, 96.

16. Kant, *Critique of Practical Reason*, 168–69.

17. Aquinas, *Summa Theologiae*, I, q. 75, a. 6.

18. Ibid., I, q. 75, a. 2, ad 3.

What inclines even me to believe in Christ's Resurrection? It is as though I play with the thought. If he did not rise from the dead, then he decomposed in the grave like any other man. *He is dead and decomposed.* In that case he is a teacher like any other and can no longer *help*; and once more we are orphaned and alone. So we have to content ourselves with wisdom and speculation. We are in a sort of hell where we can do nothing but dream, roofed in, as it were, and cut off from heaven. But if I am to be really saved,—what I need is *certainty*—not wisdom, dreams or speculation—and this certainty is faith. And faith is faith in what is needed by my *heart*, my *soul*, not my speculative intelligence. For it is my soul with its passions, as it were with its flesh and blood, that has to be saved, not my abstract mind.[19]

The hope of a Socrates and the inclination of a Wittgenstein point us beyond the grave. Our mortal, fleshly nature invites the question about death even though to answer it may well go beyond the resources of philosophy.

Owning Our Necessity

Here's the elephant in the room: *each of us must die.* Technology might help us to stave off the inevitable for a couple more years—perhaps as much as a century—but sooner or later these mortal frames will give out, and we will return to dust. Of course, we all know that one day each of us will die. But we wrongly regard that as one more objective fact among many: H_2O is the chemical symbol for water, dogs are mammals, George Washington was the first U.S. president, and I will die one day. The fact of death is rather of supreme subjective significance. No one can face death for us, but philosophers can show us just what such a confrontation might look like. What is death? What significance does it have for life? Only the shallowest of selves can be indifferent to these questions.

19. Wittgenstein, *Culture and Value*, 33.

8

If God Exists, Why Is He Hidden?

[God]

In one comic strip in the series *Calvin and Hobbes*, cartoonist Bill Watterson has his young character, Calvin, say, "This whole Santa Claus thing just doesn't make sense. Why all the secrecy? Why all the mystery? If the guy exists, why doesn't he ever show himself and prove it? And if he *doesn't* exist, what's the meaning of all this?" Hobbes says, "I dunno . . . isn't this a religious holiday?" Calvin replies, "Yeah, but actually, I've got the same questions about God."[1] Calvin isn't alone, either, but joins some good company. Bertrand Russell, a famous philosopher and atheist from the last century, was similarly baffled. Near the end of his life, students asked him whether he wasn't worried that there might be a God after all. He replied that if it turns out he's wrong, he will go up to God and complain, "You didn't give us enough evidence!"[2]

Calvin and Russell raise an excellent question: if God exists, why is he hidden? Why so little evidence?

---

1. Watterson, *Calvin and Hobbes*, December 21, 1987 (ID 67209). This cartoon can be found by going to www.amureprints.com/reprints/, checking the box next to *Calvin and Hobbes*, and entering "Santa Claus" into the Keywords bar.

2. Recounted by John Searle in *Mind, Language, and Society*, 37.

Is There Evidence for God?

To tackle this question, let's think about evidence. Neither Calvin nor Russell is bothered about whether or not Zeus exists or about any pagan deity but only about the most high God of the three great monotheistic religions. This God created the world and everything in it. For such a God, what kind of evidence would do? While we probably do not think a bigger telescope or a more powerful microscope could discover God's hiding place, we might think some scientific instrument could. But in this we are assuredly mistaken. Empirical science restricts its investigation to things in space and time, and space and time are also part of creation. Whatever the creator may be, he is certainly not spatial or temporal, and so no scientific evidence would work. In fact, if God is the creator, he is not hidden somewhere within creation. He is hidden to creatures because he is the creator and so is not part of creation.

To illustrate this, let's put ourselves in Calvin's shoes. Suppose as Calvin we ask Hobbes the question of evidence about Bill Watterson, our creator. Why is he hidden to us? Hobbes might point out that a cartoonist is by nature not part of the cartoon world he creates; by nature he is not a character in the cartoon. Evidence for the existence of Watterson is to be found in the existence of the whole comic strip, not in some spectacular aspect of the comic world he creates. Watterson is hidden to them because he is their creator. Consider an analogous case. It is no objection to the existence of black holes that they can't be seen. Their invisibility follows from their very nature as things which light cannot escape. Someone who said he wouldn't believe in a black hole unless he saw one wouldn't know what he was talking about. Similarly, it belongs to the very nature of God as creator that he be hidden.

For such a God, what kind of evidence would do? It is the world itself, the very fact that it exists, that provides evidence of that which is powerful enough and generous enough to bestow existence upon it.

Christianity of course does propose a seemingly impossible event, which Judaism and Islam find objectionable: the creator enters creation so that his creatures can better know him. He is both the creator and a creature. If Bill Watterson drew himself into the cartoon, Calvin would have evidence of his being a fellow character, but it would have to be an act of faith that he was also the creator. The nature of creator cannot be directly evidenced within creation; the cartoonist cannot be directly given to his characters. For such a God no experience is adequate, and the only approach is through testimony. We have a throng of witnesses to question: the witness of worldly beauty, goodness, and truth, which beckon us beyond themselves; the witness of the prophets; and the witness of the apostles and saints.

In a debate with Fr. Frederick Copleston, SJ, Russell denies that the existence of the world is evidence for a creator: "The universe is just there, and that's all."[3] Be that as it may, Russell at least should have realized that his desire for more evidence came from a mistake about the kind of being in question. If God is the creator, he is necessarily hidden.

Philosophers have debated just what we can know about God based on the world he creates, or whether such a God exists. Here we have sought to clear the ground for the question whether God exists by setting aside a lazy way out. The expert who denies his existence looks for the wrong kind of evidence. If the creator exists, he must be hidden, so it is necessary to seek him in order to find him.

What's the Big Deal?

Calvin asks, "If he doesn't exist, what is the meaning of all this?" The urgency of the God question is just this urgency concerning the human quest for meaning. At the beginning of the *Confessions*, Saint Augustine addresses God: "Our heart is restless until it rests in you."[4] Restlessness is part of the human condition; what will fulfill it? Our day is increasingly skeptical of traditional religious

3. Russell, "Existence of God—A Debate," 479.
4. Augustine, *Confessions* 1, 1, 1; translation modified.

answers to these questions. Nietzsche, in fact, proclaims the "death of God": what in previous ages was the most important thing now no longer carries much weight. Our secular world hardly notices something is missing, but Nietzsche argues that there is a gaping hole right in the center of our lives, and something has got to fill it.[5]

Nietzsche thinks our contemporary way of life makes belief in God impossible, because it exclusively pursues two things, business and pleasure, and religion just doesn't fit into either category.[6] Our way of life, then, puts God out of reach: "our modern, noisy, time-consuming industriousness, proud of itself, stupidly proud, educates and prepares people, more than anything else does, precisely for 'unbelief.'"[7] The most important thing is absent from our lives, because we are consumed by pleasures and are too busy to bother seeking God. Yet the question of God is not an idle curiosity. The meaning of life and the meaning of death hang in the balance.

Seeking the Hidden God

What does it mean to seek God? Pascal argues we cannot spend an afternoon or even one hundred afternoons earnestly seeking and then think we have done enough. Since everything is at stake, everything is required. He even came up with a way to market the quest to modern capitalists and their logic of calculated self-interest. According to Pascal's Wager, it is to our advantage to live as if God exists, because if we do and he does, we will win the infinite good of eternal life, and if we don't and he does, we will lose out. "Let us weigh up the gain and the loss involved in calling heads that God exists. Let us assess the two cases: if you win you win everything, if you lose you lose nothing. Do not hesitate then; wager

5. Nietzsche, *Gay Science*, §125.
6. Nietzsche, *Beyond Good and Evil*, §58.
7. Ibid.

that he does exist."[8] The ante is a finite good, and the payout is an infinite good. It is rational, then, to play and make the gamble. Pascal regards piety as a way of life which can only be understood from the inside. His wager motivates us to enter into the life so that we can understand it. As they say in Alcoholics Anonymous, "Fake it till you make it."

Of course, there are problems with the Wager. In another cartoon, Calvin announces, "Well, I've decided I *do* believe in Santa Claus, no matter how preposterous he sounds."[9]

Hobbes says, "What convinced you?"

"A simple risk analysis. I want presents, *lots* of presents. Why risk not getting them over a matter of belief? Heck, I'll believe anything they want."

Hobbes replies, "How cynically enterprising of you."

Calvin says, "It's the spirit of Christmas."

Pascal presents God, like Calvin's Santa, in an arbitrary and impersonal way, but it does appeal to our contemporary way of thinking. It is in our own private advantage to seek God unreservedly. From Pascal we can at least learn that seeking God is not a hobby but the passionate pursuit of a whole life.

What Is God?

It might seem like we should examine various proofs for God to see if they are compelling, but proofs may suggest that the default position is religious indifference and the burden of proof is on those who would counter such indifference. No one, however, should be indifferent to this question, and the burden of proof falls on each of us to find the truth and justify our position. Besides, to understand a philosophical proof would require more resources than the introductory student has at his or her disposal. What can be said

8. Pascal, *Pensées*, 123.

9. Watterson, *Calvin and Hobbes*, December 23, 1987 (ID 67211). This cartoon can be found by going to www.amureprints.com/reprints, checking the box next to *Calvin and Hobbes*, and entering "Santa Claus" in the Keywords bar.

is the following. In general, philosophers call "God" whatever they regard as highest and best. Wittgenstein writes, "The way you use the word 'God' does not show *whom* you mean—but, rather, what you mean."[10] Thales called water divine, because he thought it was the origin of all things. Different ideas of what is highest and best lead to different ideas about God. Many people live their lives as if money, fame, and power were the highest good and so divine, but philosophers put no stock in such idols.[11] Instead, philosophers have proposed different ideas about what is highest and best and consequently deserving of the name *God*.

1. *The highest nature is divine.* Socrates was put to death for not believing in the gods of the city, but he was in fact a pious fellow. Ancient philosophers criticize the view of the pagan poets because the poets anthropomorphize the gods, and because they represent the gods doing immoral things such as patricide, adultery, lying, and thieving. Instead, philosophers articulate a reasonable conception of the deity that is consistent with the good. Xenophanes, for instance, writes: "One god, greatest among all things, in no way similar to mortals either in body or in thought . . . Always he remains in the same place, moving not at all; nor is it fitting for him to go to different places at different times, but without toil he shakes all things by the thought of his mind."[12] These early philosophers call divine their ultimate principle, whether it was water, fire, being, or the good. For this position, then, the highest power of nature—and *not* human beings—is what is divine.

2. *The creator is divine.* The influence of religious revelation drove another generation of philosophers to seek a God beyond nature. These philosophers think they have good philosophical reason for thinking there is a separate origin of truth, goodness, and existence—a source that is itself supremely true, good, and existing. Thomas Aquinas writes, "God is not a part of, but above, the whole universe, possessing within himself the whole perfection

10. Wittgenstein, *Culture and Value*, 50.

11. See Thomas Aquinas, *Treatise on Happiness*, in *Summa Theologiae*, I–II, q. 1–5.

12. Kirk et al., *Presocratic Philosophers*, 169–70. Translation modified.

of the universe in a more eminent way."[13] Descartes and Leibniz think only God can explain the continued existence of things. Kant, as I noted above, thinks we have good philosophical reasons for believing in God. Many recent philosophers likewise defend this philosophical position, including Maritain, Anscombe, Stein, and Lévinas. These thinkers did not necessarily agree with each other on the philosophical reasons for this position, but they did agree on the conclusion.

3. *Humanity is divine.* Philosophers who deny a creator do not return to the identification of nature and divinity. Feuerbach, Comte, and others argue that the perfections we attribute to the creator, such as omnipotence and omniscience, are in fact properly human attributes that we project on a nonexistent entity. When we awaken to the fact that there is no creator, these attributes flow back to their true origin: ourselves. Granted that each of us alone is not all powerful and all knowing, together we are when we master nature through science and technology. These atheist humanists, then, are not really atheists, since they do have a God or highest good. It's just that they deny the creator and take *humanity* to be divine. For these thinkers, then, it is the human species taken as a whole that is God.

4. *Only some humans are divine.* Nietzsche finds the proposal of atheistic humanism to be life-denying. *Humanity* is an abstraction that averages out greatness with weakness, yielding some pale, colorless result. For Nietzsche, only the few that are well favored by nature, those with ample intelligence and will, are truly divine, and they shape the ideals that the rest of humanity follow. A more democratic version of the divinity of the few is that of Russell, who thinks that the enlightened philosopher, resigning himself to the fate of human mortality, can nonetheless think beautiful thoughts and thereby help others:

> Blind to good and evil, reckless of destruction, om-
> nipotent matter rolls on its relentless way; for Man, con-
> demned to-day to lose his dearest, to-morrow himself

13. Aquinas, *Summa Theologiae*, I, q. 61, a. 2, ad. 2.

to pass through the gate of darkness, it remains only to cherish, ere yet the blow falls, the lofty thoughts that ennoble his little day; disdaining the coward terrors of the slave of Fate, to worship at the shrine that his own hands have built; undismayed by the empire of chance, to preserve a mind free from the wanton tyranny that rules his outward life; proudly defiant of the irresistible forces that tolerate, for a moment, his knowledge and his condemnation, to sustain alone, a weary but unyielding Atlas, the world that his own ideas have fashioned despite the trampling march of unconscious power.[14]

For Russell as for Nietzsche, it is the power of the philosopher to create meaning that is truly highest and best and so deserving of the name *divine*.

5. *Each individual human is divine.* After World War II, the international philosophical superstar was Sartre, who popularized a movement called existentialism. To be human, he says, is to want to be God, and, because there is no creator, we have to realize our own divine ability and human responsibility to create ourselves. For this position, it is the power of the individual to create meaning that is divine.

The Mystery of Being

Is God greater than human beings? If so, is he something in nature or the creator of nature? If he is not greater, is he to be identified with humanity in general, some choice humans, or each human being in particular? Aristotle speaks for classical philosophy when he says that "man is not the best thing in the world."[15] He has in mind things like the stars and planets. But Pascal speaks on behalf of us moderns: "Through space the universe grasps me and swallows me up like a speck; through thought I grasp it."[16] We can no longer find something in nature divine; we know there are no

14. Russell, "Free Man's Worship," 709.

15. Aristotle, *Nicomachean Ethics* 6.7, 1141a21.

16. Pascal, *Pensées*, 29.

gods up there piloting the planets about. Are we mortals really the highest and best there is?

Against the divinity of the human, whether through atheistic humanism, philosophical supermen, or rugged individualism, Heidegger and Marcel regard the mystery of being as something higher than human beings. Heidegger poetically calls us "shepherds of being" to designate the fact that to be human means to be responsible for something other than humanity itself, to be open to the meaningfulness of things.[17] Rocks, oceans, and mountains are just there; frogs, dolphins, and antelope perceive their surroundings and interact dynamically with them; humans, by contrast, not only perceive and interact with their surroundings, they are open to the very fact that beings are as they are. No dolphins do science, write poetry, or found political institutions, but humans do all these things because they have full-blown language and the infinite possibilities it affords for understanding and making. The meaningfulness of things is not a human accomplishment, but it is something uniquely experienced by human beings. Heidegger attempts to rethink the divine not as a creator but also not as human. In fact, he characterizes the holy as the overwhelming element that emerges in the course of human life and defines it for us. Marcel, who embraced the creator as a result of his philosophical research, finds in the thick of human experience an insatiable wellspring of meaning. We cannot approach life as a problem and objectify it, because we ourselves are participating in it. I *am* only because I *belong* to a family and a lineage, only because I find myself belonging to a reality that I did not myself create.[18] Whence this world and its meaningfulness? Marcel seeks to raise the question by his philosophy, and answer it in his life. The mystery of being, then, can be held as something ultimate as in Heidegger or can open upon the creator as in Marcel. What is divine, for this view, is something greater than human beings, and it is this that makes us the kind of beings we humans are.

17. Heidegger, "Letter on Humanism," 234.
18. Marcel, "Mystery of the Family," 70–71.

Where Does That Leave Us?

Strictly speaking, no philosopher is an atheist. Even if she rejects the creator-God she affirms *some* substitute, whether that be humanity, the philosopher, the existing individual, or the mystery of being. We have to live for something if we are to live at all. The question, then, is not *whether* the divine exits, but *what kind of* thing is highest and best, and so divine. "Atheism" is not a conclusion but rather a beginning for inquiry.

We have to ask ourselves, is the taste of truth we get here, the inkling of creativity that we experience, the goodness that we achieve, and the beauty we sometimes behold indicators of something more, a foretaste of something supremely true, creative, good, and beautiful? Or are they just freakish accidents in a universe fundamentally lacking truth, creativity, goodness, and beauty? Is the existence we enjoy a taking part in something greater than ourselves, or is our existence the very best thing there is? Moreover, we find in ourselves a longing for love, and each of us has experienced not only the heartbreak of love's failures but also moments of love's reality. Can this strange love, which is a signature of the human person, be understood without recourse to a divine love that calls it into being? Or is the case that, as Augustine argues, we can love only if we have first been loved into being by love itself?[19]

Calvin wonders why God is hidden. Bill Watterson is necessarily hidden, because he is the author of the cartoon world of which Calvin is a part. But there may be another reason he is hidden: could it be, Calvin, that God is hidden because you're not looking? Even Feuerbach remarks, "The statement that one cannot know anything of the supernatural is only an excuse. God and divine things are no longer known only when one does not want

19. Augustine writes, "There is no one who doesn't love, but the question is what to love? So we are not urged [by the psalms] not to love, but to choose what we love. But what choice can we make unless we are first chosen, since we cannot love unless we are first loved?" (*Sermons*, vol. 2, 166). See also Marion, *Erotic Phenomenon*.

to know them."[20] The quest is unavoidable for each of us. What is highest and best and so deserving of the appellation, *divine*? Since philosophers disagree, we cannot avoid the bother of seeking the answer ourselves. The human desire to understand demands an answer, but the possibility of answering seems to demand nothing less than all of us—and success is not assured. Nonetheless, the ancient pagan philosopher Xenophanes provides the following reason for hope in this matter: "Yet the gods have not revealed all things to us from the beginning, but by seeking we find out better in time."[21]

20. Feuerbach, *Principles of the Philosophy of the Future*, 23.
21. Kirk et al., *Presocratic Philosophers*, 179. Translation modified.

9

Is Ignorance Bliss?

[Wisdom]

A second story comes down to us about the first philosopher, Thales of Miletus, who, you'll recall, fell down a well when he was gazing at the stars. In this second story, Thales uses his insight into nature to predict a bumper crop of olives and rents all the olive presses in the area; he then makes a killing in the olive oil market.[1] The second story, obviously fanciful, pathetically tries to hide the truth conveyed in the first. Is the search for unconventional wisdom not an impractical activity fraught with practical peril? Might it be foolish to be wise?

Further, the question may reasonably be asked: does modern society even need seekers of wisdom? Doesn't it need people skilled in business, computers, medicine, and the like? Doesn't society need human resources—technicians and workers—not thinkers? Sure, we might pay lip service to the merits of developing "critical thinking" while in school, but any form of clever reasoning would be useful in this regard; certainly not philosophy itself, for it can be much too demanding and as such is a terribly inefficient means to such an end. Society needs specialists; it has no use for philosophers.

---

1. Aristotle, *Politics* 1259a5–18.

Useless, but Desirable

Philosophy boldly admits its uselessness, but in being useless it has good company. What, for instance, is useful about happiness? What is useful about watching the sun set or seeing your favorite team win a championship? These things and many others are useless, too, because we do not want them as means to something else. Just because something is useless does not mean it is worthless. Wisdom is useless because, like happiness and all the best things in life, it is desired for its own sake.

Still, it is potentially misleading to talk about the useless quality of philosophy. It is not going to lead to a better-paying job or find a cure for cancer, but philosophy does have practical benefits. It magnifies, amplifies, and intensifies life. Its conceptual grasp serves to increase our appreciation for life and everything that goes into it. If done well, philosophy can make life better by calling attention to its wondrous character. For instance, by understanding virtue and its difficulty, we can better appreciate it when it is achieved. By understanding love, we can better realize it in our own lives. Philosophy rejects errors that make life easier for us, it prods us out of our comfort zone, and it summons us to live life with vigor.

A work of Cicero set Augustine on fire for philosophy: "All my hollow hopes suddenly seemed worthless, and with unbelievable intensity my heart burned with longing for the immortality that wisdom seemed to promise."[2] He abandoned his quest for fame and wealth to seek a wisdom that truly satisfies. He came to realize that much more is at stake in human life than passing pleasures, and he sought this something without reserve.

Philosophy affects the very way we live our everyday lives. Thoreau writes:

> There are nowadays professors of philosophy, but not philosophers. Yet it is admirable to profess because it was once admirable to live. To be a philosopher is not merely

---

2. Augustine, *Confessions*, 3, 4, 7.

to have subtle thoughts, nor even to found a school, but
so to love wisdom as to live according to its dictates, a life
of simplicity, independence, magnanimity, and trust. It is
to solve some of the problems of life, not only theoreti-
cally, but practically.[3]

Philosophy overflows into life, and life expresses itself in philosophy. "Is there any such thing as wisdom not applied to life?"[4]

So, why seek wisdom? We do so to engage reality more fully.
The quest for the true through rational inquiry can shed light on
the meaningfulness of human existence. Errors in philosophy have
the effect of disengaging us from what is real. Such errors filter into
popular culture and lead to impoverished forms of human existence. Truth in philosophy, by contrast, heightens, amplifies, and
vivifies life, enabling us to engage reality more fully. Not everyone
is called to be a professional philosopher, but everyone is called to
philosophize in one way or another. Philosophy must answer those
questions closest to the human heart, questions of meaning and
purpose. And philosophy must seek what is true for the sake of the
true simply because it is true and for no other reason.

In one sense, philosophy is useless because it doesn't help us
do anything better. But in another sense it is a most valuable inquiry, because it clarifies the aim of everything we do. Without this
knowledge, everything else is, strictly speaking, useless. If I want
to go to Times Square, it is useful to buy a plane ticket, pack my
bags, and make a hotel reservation. However, if I do not know my
destination, such things as buying a ticket, packing, and planning
are pointless. Without philosophical clarity concerning what life is
all about, nothing else can really be useful. What should I spend
my money on, why should I want to make sacrifices or be healthy,
if I don't know what all of this is for? Philosophy may be useless,
but it is supremely helpful in clarifying our good and consequently
in clarifying what is genuinely useful for the adventure that is life.

3. Thoreau, *Walden*, 12.
4. Thoreau, "Life without Principle," 355.

What Is Philosophy?

In other things we humans do, we usually don't wonder about what we're doing while we're doing it. The astronomer or biologist, for instance, simply does astronomy or biology without asking about what she's doing. The person who asks, "What is astronomy?" is on the outside of the activity. She is a beginner. Once she knows, then she can do it. It is similar for other pursuits. The baseball player does not ask what baseball is while playing it; in order to play it, he must already know.

Philosophy is peculiar in that part of doing philosophy is wondering about what it is you're doing. Philosophy is not a fixed possession but something alive, and it lives by endlessly circling about itself. Heidegger writes, "To say philosophy originates in wonder means philosophy is wondrous in its essence and becomes more wondrous the more it becomes what it really is."[5] This does not mean we can't gain clarity, but it does mean that philosophy cannot happen in a textbook or database since it dies when it becomes a result.

With this in mind we can hazard the following: philosophy, the quest for unconventional wisdom, inwardly intensifies life through understanding. Philosophical terms, while seemingly dry and lifeless on their own, have the ability to make our lives bear fruit. Conversely, the wrong kind of notions choke the vine and lead to a paltry harvest. Truth, goodness, and beauty are the sunlight, fertilizer, and water for human life. Conventional wisdom has us wither away, but philosophy can really get the juices flowing.

Take the *conventional* view. If science knows all there is to know, I need only turn to the scientific experts; I do not have to think for myself. If beauty is merely a projection of my own fancy, there will be little to encounter and savor in things. If I think goodness is pleasure, I can just lose myself in the present. If I think meaning is something to choose for myself, I will have nothing to search for and struggle to adopt. If love is disguised self-hatred, then I will not feel motivated to practice it. If death makes me feel

5. Heidegger, *Basic Questions*, 141.

bad, I can distract myself with trifles. If the burden of proof is on the divine and not on me, I do not need to trouble myself seeking.

Now take the *unconventional* view. Scientific experts do not know all there is to know, so I have to trouble myself inquiring. Beauty is not merely subjective, so I have to bring my fancies into conformity with what is really there in reality and allow myself to be transformed in the process. There is more to goodness than pleasure, so I have to choose some suffering and struggle to develop virtue. Meaning can be discovered and realized, so I have a lot of work to do. Love enlarges my life, so I should allow it to shape me. If my stance towards death measures my stance towards life, I had better confront it. If the burden is on me to find God, then I am not allowed a day's rest.

Now I know that to an onlooker, philosophy may appear abstract and divorced from life. But to the one who undertakes to philosophize, life itself is enriched. When Socrates says the unexamined life is not worth living, he means that the search for unconventional wisdom is a most wholesome joy. As he lay dying, he reminds his friends, "Do not be careless!"[6] Care for truth, goodness, and beauty above wealth and reputation and you will live a life that is fully alive, richly meaningful, and marvelously pleasurable. As Descartes puts it, philosophy awakens us to the beauty and truth of things: "Living without philosophizing is exactly like having one's eyes closed without ever trying to open them; and the pleasure of seeing everything which our sight reveals is in no way comparable to the satisfaction accorded by knowledge of the things which philosophy enables us to discover."[7] For philosophy, like art and religion, continually recovers the insight that something essential is at stake in life. As Wittgenstein says, "The delight I take in my thoughts is delight in my own strange life."[8]

---

6. Plato, *Phaedo* 118a; translation modified. See Madison, "Have We Been Careless with Socrates' Last Words?," 435–36.

7. Descartes, *Principles of Philosophy*, 180.

8. Wittgenstein, *Culture and Value*, 22.

How to Read a Bit of Philosophy

1. Prepare Yourself to Read.

Get ready. Are you well rested? If you're lethargic, take a walk. Don't attempt to read philosophy when you're starving or when you've just had a large meal. You'll need to marshal your full powers of concentration. Also, don't do too much in one sitting, but take breaks to clear your mind and consider what you've been reading.

("The intellect wills the primary essence because otherwise the first and second causes are considered abstractly and not concretely in their manifold of meaning." Philosophy will read like this bit of nonsense if you're too tired to follow what's going on.)

2. While You Read, Willfully Suspend Your Disbelief.

Philosophers have a peculiar manner of speaking, and our first reaction is likely to dismiss what they are saying as absurd. It strikes us as simply unbelievable. By contrast, when we see a movie, even when it includes all sorts of fantastic things like Ring-wraiths and trolls, we spontaneously believe that in the world the movie depicts, these things are true. Only in bad movies when something violates the realm of the probable do we have to suspend our disbelief. Reading philosophy is like watching a bad movie: you have to resist your initial disbelief.

(For instance, what is our first response when we hear Thales, the first philosopher, declare, "All is water"? Doesn't he sound like he's off his rocker?)

3. While You Read, Identify and Underline the Philosopher's Proposals.

Philosophers typically make their own proposals by contrasting them with other possible proposals and giving reasons to justify their own. The following questions may prove helpful in identifying what the philosopher is claiming.

(a) What is (are) the philosopher's main point(s), and how does he or she go about proving it (them)?

(b) What are the key distinctions the philosopher makes, and what do they mean?

(c) What positions does he or she reject and why?

(d) What positions does he or she affirm and why?

Be sure to underline the text, number the steps in an argument, and make copious marginal notes for key points. You must take ownership of what the philosopher says, and you do so by identifying and underlining.

(For Thales, we have little to go on, but when he says "All is water" he is contrasting his position with other claims we could make, such as "All is fire" (Heraclitus). When Aristotle later says that the pre-Socratic thinkers only discovered matter, he has in mind three other causes they missed: formal, final, and efficient, and he provides reasons for including these as well.)

4. While You Read, Try to Make Sense of the Philosopher's Proposals.

Even before asking whether or not it's true, try to figure out how the thinker's proposal could possibly make sense so that someone who is presumably sane and perhaps insightful could think it is true.

(For instance, Thales must not mean that everything, including rocks, is watery or that H_2O is the universal building block of

all things. How then can his declaration appear sensible? Perhaps Thales is using familiar words in a new philosophical way and is asking us to consider the unity of the whole cosmos: in a way all is one. Perhaps he chooses "water" to signify the unity because of the ancient belief, shared by Genesis, that water filled the heavens above and the oceans below, providing the ultimate context in which terrestrial things emerge.)

5. After You Read, Ask Whether and How the Proposals Are True.

Once you've taken steps 2, 3, and 4 you're ready for the payoff. Imagine for a second you skipped them and went right to 5; then you could only honestly say, "While I do not know or understand what the philosopher is saying, I think it is false." But this wouldn't make any sense, though it happens all the time when people talk about philosophers. Only if we try to believe can we possibly understand, and only if we understand do we gain the ability to judge whether something is true or false. And often it is somewhere in between: what the philosopher says is in some sense true, in another false.

(Thales is right to think there is a unity to the cosmos, but he is wrong to think water can conceptualize this unity. Parmenides, in fact, will happen on the right concept to name all things: "being.")

Summary

Compare my list to the following helpful instructions given by Descartes: "I should like the reader first of all to go quickly through the whole book like a novel, without straining his attention too much or stopping at the difficulties which may be encountered. The aim should be merely to ascertain in a general way which matters I have dealt with. After this, if he finds that these matters deserve to be examined and he has the curiosity to ascertain their causes, he may read the book a second time in order to observe how my arguments follow. But if he is not always able to see this fully, or if he does not understand all the arguments, he would not give up at once. He should merely mark with a pen the places where he finds the difficulties and continue to read on to the end without a break. If he then takes up the book for the third time, I venture to think he will now find the solutions to most of the difficulties he marked before; and if any still remain, he will discover their solution on a final re-reading."[1] Notice that the founder of modern philosophy immodestly neglects step 5, but no philosopher, not even Descartes, gets it 100 percent right.

What to Read

To pursue the themes of this book, consider reading some of the following texts.

Plato

The Athenians put Socrates to death for questioning conventional wisdom. In the *Apology*, Plato provides the defense that Socrates made at his trial (here "apology" does not mean "I am sorry" but instead "here's why I am right.") The Athenians did not buy it, and put Socrates to death anyway. In the *Republic*, Plato provides his own defense of Socrates and the philosophical way of life by arguing that philosophy combats the native tendency of the human heart to seek one's own private advantage. Philosophy counters the maxim that "might makes right" by showing the priority of the common good. Ideal political leaders would be philosophers, who know what the common good is and rule for its sake, not for their private advantage. Plato argues that doing and being good is its own reward, and doing bad and being bad is its own punishment, since the good person has a harmonious soul, and the bad one is tormented by his or her own desires. In the *Phaedo*, Plato provides a stylized account of Socrates's last conversation, which culminates

1. Descartes, *Principles of Philosophy*, 185.

in his dramatic death scene. Socrates explains to his companions why he is cheerful by laying out the case for hope in an afterlife.

Aristotle

In the *Nicomachean Ethics*, Aristotle points out that while everyone agrees that they want to be happy, there is quite a bit of disagreement over just where happiness is to be found: in money, pleasure, power, or what have you. Aristotle argues that human happiness consists in developing our natural ability to be virtuous. He thinks that happiness is an objective state of human flourishing involving such moral virtues as courage, justice, and moderation. He also holds that intellectual development is essential as well, and he points to prudence, art, science, and wisdom as key components of human happiness. The crown of the ethical life is good friends. The virtuous person can have profound and lasting friendships; others can only have friends based on the mutual exchange of pleasure or utility.

St. Augustine

In the *Confessions*, Augustine recounts his search for wisdom. His parents had groomed him for a life of political power and influence, and he also fell into a life of sensual delights. However, his priorities began to change when he read a book by Cicero that identified the meaninglessness of conventional wisdom and such goods as honor and bodily pleasure. Augustine began to hunger for much more, but it would take encountering followers of Plato and the preaching of St. Ambrose to discover where wisdom can actually be found. In *On Free Choice of the Will*, Augustine recounts conversations concerning such topics as freedom, truth, and God.

St. Thomas Aquinas

Aquinas's *Treatise on Human Happiness* is a small section of a massive textbook he wrote for graduate students titled *Summa Theologiae*. He argues that happiness cannot consist in such goods as money, power, honor, or pleasure, but must come in fulfilling our human appetite for truth. In *Summa Contra Gentiles*, book 1, he sketches a philosophical ascent from this created world to its uncreated cause.

Rousseau

Rousseau became famous with his *First Discourse on the Arts and Sciences*, in which he argues that the modern way of life, founded on science and technology, will not make us better or happier, but in fact will have the opposite effect. Technological civilization causes us to live in the eyes of others and to treasure appearance over reality so that virtue is no longer our concern. In the *Second Discourse on the Origin of Inequality*, he makes bold to claim that the march of civilization in fact shackles our liberty.

Kant

Challenged by Rousseau, Kant defends the development of freedom in such essays as "Speculative Beginning of Human History." He agrees with Rousseau that freedom, not science and technology, constitutes our highest good, but he thinks that awareness of freedom develops through human history. Kant says that freedom is not a feeling, as it was for Rousseau, but the ability to will the universal moral law, a point he develops in *Groundwork for the Metaphysics of Morals*.

Kierkegaard

In *The Present Age*, Kierkegaard ridicules the abstraction of modern life. Instead of engaging in the essential task of becoming good, the media want us to gossip and fear the opinion of others. In *Either/Or*, Kierkegaard sketches two paths: a path of fulfillment through passing pleasures and a path of fulfillment through becoming good, and he leaves it to readers to choose between them. In *Concluding Unscientific Postscript*, he argues that in such questions as the meaning of life and death, each of us must personally be engaged in the highest degree possible. A good anthology, such as *The Essential Kierkegaard* or *A Kierkegaard Anthology* will include judicious extracts from these works.

Thoreau

In *Walden*, Thoreau recounts his days of solitude amid nature on the shores of Walden Pond in Concord, Massachusetts. He calls into question the business of everyday life, and he invites readers to find joy in a life of simplicity and contemplation. The essay "Life without Principle," concentrates the wisdom of *Walden* into a few pages.

Nietzsche

In *Philosophy in the Tragic Age of the Greeks*, Nietzsche gives an account of the first philosophers as engaged in seeking wisdom. In *Advantage and Disadvantage of History for Life*, he argues that knowledge in general is detrimental to the task of living. We are not databases but living beings with interests; we hunger for wisdom, not information.

Do I Have to Be a Skeptic?

The poet Alexander Pope wrote a cautionary verse relevant to the study of philosophy: "A little learning is a dangerous thing; / Drink deep, or taste not the Pierian spring."[1] Typically Philosophy 101 has the effect of inducing a bizarre and unnatural doubt, which is called skepticism. The noted psychologist Steven Pinker, writing in *Time* magazine, remarked that every intro to philosophy course causes us to wonder whether other people are mindless zombies.[2] Is this really what philosophy is all about? Invoking exotic doubt? The culprit is the most readable philosopher of all time, René Descartes.

As a professor I must confess teaching Descartes is extremely enjoyable. He brings students into a state of extreme bafflement, wondering how they can be sure of anything; and then—*voila!*—he dramatically unveils the impossibility of doubting one's own existence in the most quoted line in philosophy: "I think, therefore I exist." Rather than resort to the dreary abstraction of most philosophy, Descartes masterfully appeals to the imagination, and philosophy teachers, like anyone else, want to entertain. Besides, Descartes happens to be the most influential and readable modern philosopher. Teachers of Philosophy 101 or writers of introductory books accordingly put the so-called Problem of the External

---

1. Pope, "Essay on Criticism," lines 215–16.
2. Pinker, "Brain," 70.

World out in front. No one can be indifferent to such a problem, surely.

Descartes tries to motivate universal doubt in several stages. His strategy is to reject all that could be false in order to find what cannot possibly be false.

First, senses sometimes deceive. For example, a straw in water appears broken, but it is not. Descartes says that if our senses have misled us once, prudence demands us to be suspicious of them all the time. Fool me once, shame on you; fool me twice, shame on me.

Second, instead of really reading this book, we might right now be dreaming where all sorts of false things appear true. If it's ever happened that we were dreaming when we thought we weren't, Descartes says we can't be sure at this particular moment whether we're asleep or awake.

Third, reasoning sometimes errs. We've all made mistakes in math without realizing it. Our present reasoning, then, might be mistaken.

Fourth, Descartes goes nuclear. Not only might we be mistaken here and there, but it could be that we are mistaken all the time about everything. How's that? There could be an all-powerful evil genius deceiving us. It is an extremely remote possibility, but how can we rule it out for sure?

Having deployed these four considerations, Descartes plays his ace. What cannot be doubted is: *I think* (I am aware), *therefore I am*. Even if an evil deceiver deceives me about all the content of my thought, he cannot deceive me about this: while I am deceived, I must exist. What about, *I ski, therefore I am*? *I drink, therefore I am*? *I eat pistachios, therefore I am*? These statements could be doubted, but awareness cannot be doubted, because it is the condition for doubting. To see this clearly, consider something my four-year-old said: "Grampa, pretend that you are a dinosaur that doesn't exist." Surely, Grandpa could pretend to be a dinosaur and he could pretend to be sleeping, but he could not pretend that he didn't exist. There's no way to do that, because existence is the ground for all of our activities, including pretending. If I think, I must exist.

Where Descartes goes from here is to prove God's existence and to bring about a universal mathematical model for nature, suited for the advance of our technological mastery. But what sticks in undergraduate minds is just this universal doubt and the fact we seem stuck in the first-person, egocentric predicament. From the confines of our consciousness, we peer suspiciously out at the world.

David Hume, the most famous skeptic of modern times, shows what happens when Cartesian doubt runs its course. Hume finds himself hopelessly confused, because he unleashes radical doubt while denying the remedy of a good God to guarantee our knowledge: "The *intense* view of these manifold contradictions and imperfections in human reason has so wrought upon me, and heated my brain, that I am ready to reject all belief and reasoning, and can look upon no opinion even as more probable or likely than another."[3] He tells us that under the skeptical spell, he falls into "philosophical melancholy and delirium" and only finds relief through diversions: "I dine, I play a game of back-gammon, I converse, and am merry with my friends; and when after three or four hour's amusement, I wou'd return to these speculations, they appear so cold, and strain'd, and ridiculous, that I cannot find in my heart to enter into them any further."[4] The example of Hume shows that when doubt gets out of hand, philosophy becomes something monstrous; rather than intensify life, it bleaches life of meaning.

We come, then, to an important question: if we are to be philosophical, must we be skeptical? Now, there is an ingredient of doubt in the *search* for wisdom; we have to be somewhat skeptical about conventional wisdom to want to seek *un*conventional wisdom. But the kind of doubt recommended by Descartes is not necessary for philosophy. In fact, contemporary philosophers have

3. Hume, *Treatise on Human Nature*, 268–69.
4. Ibid., 269.

come to the consensus that it is a dead end. Not only is it unfruitful, but it is also incoherent. In what way?

As Aristotle among the ancient Greeks had already realized, we cannot prove at this moment that we are not dreaming, and people who ask for such proofs lack wisdom.[5] Every proof must begin with a premise, and the first premises of things cannot themselves be proved. If proposition A is used to prove proposition B, then proposition B cannot be used to prove proposition A. It is a mark of wisdom to know what needs to be proven and what cannot be proven, because it is impossible for everything to be proven. Being aware of the world is a basic presupposition of experience that cannot be called into question. This does not make world access merely a matter of belief. Beliefs can be meaningfully doubted, but not world access.

Heidegger influentially maintains that to be human means to be in a world with others. The skeptical problematic, according to which we might be all alone in our consciousness, with no access to the world, betrays a colossal misunderstanding of what it means to be human.[6] As Descartes proceeds to make claims about the truth and publish his findings for others to read, it becomes clear that there is an almost humorous gap between his theoretical self-understanding and his actual engagement in the world with others. Skepticism is inhuman and unlivable.

Wittgenstein also brilliantly calls attention to the impossibility of universal doubt. While Descartes attempts to doubt everything he had ever been told, he does not and can not doubt the language in which he expresses his doubt. Language is a creature of the public world. We cannot meaningfully doubt that world while using language, nor can we get by without language. Denying access to the public world, then, is a fool's errand. Moreover, doubts must be motivated by a belief: I begin to doubt the salesman because I believe he may be lying. Consequently, "a doubt

---

5. Aristotle, *Metaphysics* 4.6.

6. Heidegger, *Being and Time*, 246–47.

that doubted everything would not be a doubt."[7] A universal doubt is impossible, because it could not be motivated as a doubt.

Descartes did not doubt for the sake of doubting. He wanted to bring about a foundation for the new science and its technological prowess. To use Descartes's own metaphor, doubt is a disease dispatched in order to sell the cure. As he wrote in reply to Hobbes, "I was not looking for praise when I set out these arguments [for doubting]; but I think I could not have left them out, any more than a medical writer can leave out the description of a disease when he wants to explain how it can be cured."[8] In the same vein, I would like to offer this appendix as an inoculation against the disease, thereby rendering superfluous the Cartesian cure. You can be philosophical without being a skeptic.

7. Wittgenstein, *On Certainty*, §450.
8. Descartes, "Third Replies (to Hobbes)," 121.

Philosophers and Their Guiding Stars

How many philosophers does it take to screw in a lightbulb? It depends on the philosopher. Socrates would maintain that he didn't know how to screw it in, and he would question everybody else to show that they didn't really know either. Plato would contemplate the eternal, unchanging lightbulb and ignore the darkness around him. Hume would deny the causal connection between burned-out bulb and darkness, and so would do nothing. Nietzsche would smash the bulb to pieces with a hammer, Wittgenstein would draw a light bulb pictogram in his notebook, and Heidegger would say only a god can change it now. (If you don't want to be on the outside of these inside jokes, read this Glossary.)

⁂

Gertrude Elizabeth Margaret Anscombe (1919–2001), British, was a student and later a friend of the philosopher Ludwig Wittgenstein. She married the philosopher Peter Geach, whom she met while converting to Catholicism, and they had seven children. She made major contributions to action theory and ethics, which led her to reject the morality of contraception as well as Truman's bombing of Hiroshima. She is buried right next to Wittgenstein.

St. Thomas Aquinas (1224/5–1274), Italian, the younger son of a noble family, was supposed to become the abbot of a wealthy monastery, but against his family's wishes he left the easy life to join a band of beggars devoted to preaching. He studied under St. Albert the Great and synthesized St. Augustine's thought with the newly rediscovered philosophy of Aristotle. Though he had a wide girth, when he walked through the countryside, peasants would leave their work to marvel at his beauty. Famous for getting lost in thought, he would have to be brought back to his senses with a bell or a tug on his habit. After he wrote the *Summa Contra Gentiles*, he composed his masterpiece, the *Summa Theologiae*, which he dictated to several secretaries at the same time. Near the end of his life, he abruptly stopped work on the *Summa* after a mystical experience, saying, "All that I have written is as straw compared to the things that I have seen." He understood the pursuit of wisdom as beneficial, because it joins us in friendship to the God who is wisdom itself.

Hannah Arendt (1906–1975), German, studied with Heidegger and became a prominent political philosopher. Due to her Jewish heritage she had to flee Germany and came to the U.S. in 1941. Her writings grapple with the evil of Nazism and totalitarianism. She also thought long and hard about the human person as both an active and a contemplative being.

Aristotle (384–322 BC), Greek, studied with Plato for 20 years before founding his own school. He studied biology, did dissections, and wrote extensively on the human person, political life, and the nature of reality. His masterpiece on what it means to be human, *Nicomachean Ethics*, details the quest for happiness and the virtues, both moral and intellectual, needed to obtain it. Friendship crowns the virtuous life. Only a beast or a god would have no need of friends.

St. Augustine (354–430), Roman, from North Africa, was groomed for a life of politics, but his life changed after reading a work of philosophy by Cicero. He abandoned his quest for power and instead sought wisdom, and he found it in Plato and in biblical revelation. He proclaimed, "You have made us for yourself, O Lord, and our hearts are restless until they rest in you." He wrote the *Confessions*, the first autobiography ever, along with many philosophical and theological works. In the last century, his writings inspired Husserl, Heidegger, and Wittgenstein, among other philosophers. Augustine ardently sought wisdom, and he found that his friendships with such people as St. Ambrose, St. Alypius and even his mother, St. Monica, furthered him in his quest. Friendship, he realized, is the best thing in this life.

Marcus Aurelius (121–180), Roman emperor, who wrote a book called *Meditations* in which he promoted Stoic principles of seeking happiness apart from the passions.

Auguste Comte (1798–1857), French, posited three historical ages: religion, philosophy, and science. The first two are now obsolete in view of the success of the last stage. Comte called for a new humanity founded on altruism, with scientists as the high priests.

René Descartes (1596–1650), French, the founder of modern philosophy, was a brilliant mathematician who bridged geometry and algebra and laid a foundation for modern science and technology. He refuted radical doubt with the self-evident proposition, "I think, therefore I am." After him, philosophy takes consciousness, not the public world of perceived nature, as its starting point, although the last two centuries have found many thinkers seeking a way out of this predicament. He wished to make us "masters and possessors of nature" in order to make life easier through technology (think of the washing machine and the combine, not to mention epidurals and pain medication), to make life longer (think of the wonders of present medical science), and to make us feel better through pharmaceuticals (think of antidepressants).

Ludwig Feuerbach (1804–1872), German, whose name means "River of Fire," dissolved theology and philosophy into anthropology and declared a religion of humanity. His elimination of God from philosophy influenced Marx.

Georg Wilhelm Friedrich Hegel (1770–1831), German, said the Owl of Minerva flies at dusk, it was now dusk, and so it was time for wisdom to spread her wings. Dissolving Christian theology into philosophy, he argued that world history, culture, and religion exhibit a rational progression that culminates in the self-realization of the Absolute at the very moment Hegel lived. Though his system proved wildly popular for a generation it came to breed distrust of all speculation in subsequent philosophers, who instead clamored to change the world. Hegel sought to comprehend everything, God included, within an all-embracing, closed system. Kierkegaard said the only thing the grand system left out was the philosopher who dreamed it up. Forgetting the philosopher is a fatal omission for philosophy.

Martin Heidegger (1889–1976), German, rekindled the ancient question of being and argued for the significance of being human. He claimed that technology dominates our conventional way of thinking so that even when we are faced with problems caused by technology we look to technological solutions (such as so-called "green technology") rather than changes in how we live and think. In the face of the all-consuming logic of modern technology, he said, "Only a god can save us now."

Heraclitus the Obscure (c. 500 BC), Greek, turned philosophical attention to the way to live life, and he wove together insight into nature and insight into the right way to live. A cosmic principle of order, which he called "logos" or reason, gives us insight into the structure of things and a truly divine way of life. Against Parmenides, he argued that change and rest imply each other, so he affirmed both the reality of change and its underlying order. A self-proclaimed disciple, Cratylus, botched Heraclitus's careful balance and unintelligibly proclaimed a doctrine of universal flux: everything is constantly changing. Heraclitus said you cannot step into the exact same river twice because new waters are always flowing, but Cratylus said you cannot step into the same river even once!

David Hume (1711–1776), Scottish, rejected Cartesian rationalism while holding to the way of doubt. He analyzed the idea of causality and argued it is not based on an insight or experience but on a feeling entrenched by habit; his analysis undermined not only traditional philosophy and theology but also the crown jewel of modernity: Newtonian physics. He also countered traditional ideas about virtue by insisting that we are powerless to do anything contrary to our passions. A brilliant analytic thinker, he nonetheless was a cheerless philosopher.

Edmund Husserl (1859–1938), German, pioneered a way of philosophizing called phenomenology, which seeks to trace back all our ideas to the way they are initially given in our experience. Against the Cartesian isolation of consciousness, he insisted that thought is always *of* something; it always targets something in the world. A mathematician by training, he focused principally on the way mathematics, logic, and language are rooted in experience while remaining timelessly valid. He regarded philosophy as a rigorous science and an endless, collaborative task in which phenomenologists would investigate all dimensions of human experience.

Immanuel Kant (1724–1804), German, continues to be the most influential late modern philosopher. Shocked by Rousseau, he struggled to work out a notion of moral progress; scared by Hume, he ingeniously saved the idea of causality—and modern

Newtonian physics—by making causality a necessary law of consciousness. He said philosophers ask four major questions. What can I know? What ought I to do? What can I hope for? What is man? His three major works answer the first three questions. The *Critique of Pure Reason* identifies the human limits of truth. The *Critique of Practical Reason* lays forth the absolute obligations of the good. The Categorical Imperative articulates our fundamental obligation to respect the kingdom of ends, that is, the communion of persons. The *Critique of Judgment* talks about the interplay of beauty and nature and how that points to a possible fulfillment of human hopes. The question about human nature comes to the fore in each of these investigations, and it is a question that Kant bequeaths to subsequent thinkers. Kant's schedule was so regular that it is said the housewives of his native city set their clocks according to his daily walks.

Søren Kierkegaard (1813–1855), Danish, saw the state of Christendom in his day and took as his task making Christians Christian again. In the process, he contrasted the meaningless life of pleasure with the meaningful life of virtue and sacrifice, before introducing the highest kind of life in religious devotion to the Absolute. He was a thinker who savored paradox as the way to instill fire in the soul, and he brought out the paradoxical juxtaposition of the timeless and the temporal in Christianity. Kierkegaard is one of the most widely read philosophers and justly so, for he writes with insight and wit.

Gottfried Wilhelm Leibniz (1646–1716), German, codiscovered the calculus with Newton, and developed a philosophy of being compatible with modern mathematical physics. He formulated the philosophical question concerning the radical origination of all things: "Why is there something rather than nothing?" He argued that the question leads us to a being simple and unoriginated, whom he called God.

Emmanuel Lévinas (1906–1995), Lithuanian, devoted his philosophy to the roots of our ethical obligations. Horrified with the death camps of World War II, he argued that philosophy itself was partially to blame, because it had failed to bring to light the responsibility each of us has for the other. He saw a kind of egoism run through much of philosophy, and he tried to tear it open in such experiences as love.

John Locke (1632–1704), British, developed a theory of political revolution that was influential in the American founding. He argued that natural law is more fundamental than political law; consequently, if a political power, say a king, imposes civil laws that violate natural laws, he in effect declares war on them. In justice, they must overthrow his rule as a matter of self-defense. For Locke, true freedom or liberty requires natural law and reason; without these, we fall prey to a kind of slavery to whim that he calls license.

Gabriel Marcel (1889–1973), French, philosophized about the significance of concrete human situations and experiences, such as love, family, hope, and technology. He contrasted the technical, problem-solving mode of thinking with the contemplative, recollective mode proper to philosophy. He thought that we lived in a "broken world" and that we had to recover the mystery of being for our lives to make sense.

Jean-Luc Marion (1946–), French, puzzled over the loss of meaning in the modern world and found a clue in the difference between an idol and an icon. The idol is something we idolize; in it we meet with ourselves. The icon, by contrast, is something that disrupts us and pulls us beyond ourselves. Marion thinks that love goes the way of the icon. Love offers the only means of finding meaning in the world.

Jacques Maritain (1882–1973), French, made a suicide pact with his girlfriend, Raïssa, unless they could discover the meaning of life. Fortunately, they discovered philosophy, which countered the meaningless scientism of the day. They married and soon converted to Catholicism. Jacques became a leading interpreter of the philosophical thought of Thomas Aquinas. In his political philosophy, he argued for the dignity of the human person and the priority of the common good, and he participated in the drafting of the United Nations Universal Declaration of Human Rights. He also published on knowledge, nature, being, and God. Raïssa wrote a moving memoir titled *We Have Been Friends Together.*

John Stuart Mill (1806–1873), British, had a rigorous education at the hands of his father, who introduced him to Greek at age three and desired that his son should develop into a philosopher according to the pattern he set. As a young man, Mill fell into depression only to discover that his father's approach, focused only on logic, had neglected to give him a sense of what makes life livable. Reading the poetry of Wordsworth disclosed to him new possibilities. He later published works on logic, ethics, and social theory.

Friedrich Nietzsche (1844–1900), German, suffered the demise of the Western way of life, but he did so with decided good cheer. Music is the key to the good life, and his writings have a certain inimitable style and a tempo that is infectious. Philosophizing "with a hammer," Nietzsche demolished traditional ideas about God, reality, and the common good, and advocated instead a view of the philosophical soul as the raison d'être of the whole world. Accordingly, he thought popular presentations of philosophy, such as this one, are worthless in principle, since they try to make available to the many what can only be understood by the few. The ample power of the philosopher to make meaning allows him to proclaim "yes" to existence and then break into song. His *Beyond Good and Evil* and *Thus Spoke Zarathustra* present his mature thinking in prose, argument, and occasional verse.

Parmenides (c. 500 BC), Greek, happened upon the right concept for philosophy, "being." Whereas Thales had said all things were "water," Anaximander "infinite," Anaximenes "air," Heraclitus "fire," Parmenides reasoned that everything *is*. Moreover, if everything is (present tense), then nothing can come to be (future tense) or cease to be (past tense). Parmenides boldly denied the reality of change and affirmed the divine reality of eternal being.

Blaise Pascal (1623–1662), French, after pioneering the probability calculus, had a mystical experience "of the God of Abraham, Isaac, and Jacob, not the God of the philosophers" and subsequently turned his considerable intellect toward motivating his contemporaries to seek God. His *Pensées* is essential reading concerning the dignity of the human being, the troublesome distractions of everyday life, and the need for redemption. In it, he famously formulates his Wager, which argues on the basis of probability that it is eminently reasonable to seek God, since what we wage, our life, is finite, but the possible payout, eternal life, infinite. We have little to lose and everything to gain.

Giovanni Pico della Mirandola (1463–1494), Italian, a brilliant Renaissance thinker, sought to reconcile all conflicting viewpoints into one sweeping view of things. Philosophers generally come in two kinds. One wants to say that every other philosopher is wrong. The other wants to say that everybody is right, and he has to come up with a clever way of reconciling their differences. Pico is of the latter kind.

Plato (c. 429–347 BC), Greek, philosophy's most influential thinker and writer, was struck by the enigmatic figure of Socrates, whose death at the hands of his fellow Athenians made Plato suspicious of the mob and defensive of the philosophical way of life. Many of Plato's dialogues involve Socrates as a central character, even though Plato generally uses the character as a mouthpiece for his own ideas. Influenced by Parmenides, who denied change, and Heraclitus, who saw change everywhere, Plato distinguished the eternal realm of meaning from the flux of the sensible realm. In the *Republic*, Plato argues for the primacy of the common good against the conventional view that might makes right. In the *Symposium*, he speculates that the meaning of life is love and that the meaning of love is new life. Plato saw beauty and the good as guiding stars for human life. Moved by beauty, we seek the good. In doing good, we become good. In becoming good, we become divine and blessedly happy.

Plotinus (204–270), Egyptian, developed Plato's ideas some 600 years after his death. Plotinus urged his students to turn within and above in order to become aware of the divine origin of beauty, truth, and goodness.

Jean-Jacques Rousseau (1712–1778), Swiss, became famous for winning an essay contest answering the question of "whether progress in science and technology has led to progress in morality." Against conventional wisdom, he argued that scientific and technological advances do not lead to moral progress; in fact they lead to a regress in morals, because we are so busy keeping up with the Joneses, distracted by our things and our mastery of nature, that we forget ourselves and the hard work of cultivating virtue.

Bertrand Russell (1872–1970), British, developed modern mathematical logic before speaking out on social and religious issues. This exceptional logician found logic, the science of clear thinking, extremely difficult due to the paradoxes it generates and the counterexamples it runs up against. He often said to his friend, the philosopher Ludwig Wittgenstein, "Logic's hell!"

Jean-Paul Sartre (1905–1980), French, practiced phenomenology and wrote plays, becoming hugely popular after World War II, when people were provoked to seek meaning for their lives. In the popular essay "Existentialism Is a Humanism," he argues that though there is no natural meaning to life, we are free to create meaning for ourselves. In the famous play *No Exit*, he opines that hell is the presence of other people.

Max Scheler (1874–1928), German, was an intuitive thinker with a robust personal presence. He reflected on the human person and collaborated with Husserl in the founding of phenomenology.

Socrates (c. 470–399 BC), Greek, refocused philosophy from the study of nature to the study of human nature. Famously ugly and poor, he nonetheless captivated his fellow Athenians, who began to wonder just what was so moving about a man neither beautiful nor rich. He claimed to know nothing except the art of love, and he fancied himself a midwife who sought to bring truth out of all those he encountered. After revealing that many influential figures, regarded as wise by conventional standards, in fact knew nothing, Socrates was put to death by his fellow Athenians. He only wrote some poetry, which has not survived, but Plato, his most famous student, wrote down some of his thoughts in the form of dialogues. Among these is the *Apology*, Socrates's defense at his trial, in which Socrates' memorably maintains, "The unexamined life is not worth living."

St. Edith Stein (1891–1942), German, was a Jewish student of Edmund Husserl. She converted to Catholicism, and she sought to combine Husserl's thought with Thomas Aquinas's. After becoming a Carmelite nun, she was arrested by the Nazis and died in Auschwitz.

Thales of Miletus (c. 585 BC), Greek, the first Western philosopher, criticized pagan religious myth and began inquiry into the nature of things. He posited water as the divine cause of all things.

Henry David Thoreau (1817–1862), American, sought a simple way of life in nature, apart from the bustle of city dwelling. His *Walden* is a contemplative journey into nature; though the book is slow, it harbors the power of reversing one's priorities in order to pursue a thoughtful life.

Ludwig Wittgenstein (1889–1951), Austrian, collaborated with Russell in formulating the mathematical logic. Thinking he had solved all philosophical problems, he retired to the countryside to teach grammar to schoolchildren. Eventually he realized his error, and he struggled to come up with an alternative to his earlier thought. His later writings are cryptic but intense and often enjoyable. (They contain, for instance, the occasional pictogram, such as the infamous "duck-rabbit," which can be viewed as either a duck or a rabbit.) *Culture and Value* collects his thoughts on religion and art, and *On Certainty* his thoughts on the incoherence of skepticism.

Xenophanes (c. 570–475 BC), Greek, criticized pagan religion as anthropomorphic. (He said that if cows worshiped, they would say that the gods looked like cows.) He also introduced a philosophical approach to God as the highest principle of nature.

Bibliography

Arendt, Hannah. *The Life of the Mind*. Vol. 2, *Willing*. San Diego: Harcourt Brace Jovanovich, 1978.

Aristotle. "Fragments." In *The Complete Works of Aristotle: The Revised Oxford Translation*, 2:2389–465. Edited by Jonathan Barnes. 2 vols. Bollingen Series 71/2. Princeton: Princeton University Press, 1984.

———. *Metaphysics*. In *The Basic Works of Aristotle*, edited by Richard McKeon, 689–926. Lifetime Library. New York: Random House, 1941.

———. *Nicomachean Ethics*. In *The Basic Works of Aristotle*, edited by Richard McKeon, 935–1112. Lifetime Library. New York: Random House, 1941.

———. *Poetics*. In *The Basic Works of Aristotle*, edited by Richard McKeon, 1455–87. Lifetime Library. New York: Random House, 1941.

———. *Politics*. In *The Basic Works of Aristotle*, edited by Richard McKeon, 1127–1316. Lifetime Library. New York: Random House, 1941.

Augustine, Saint. *Confessions*. Translated by Maria Boulding. Hyde Park, NY: New City, 1997.

———. *Sermons*. Vol. 2. Translated by Edmund Hill. Edited by John E. Rotelle. Brooklyn: New City, 1990.

Austen, Jane. *The Novels of Jane Austen: Pride and Prejudice*, vol. 1. London: Richards, 1898.

Boswell, James. "An Account of My Last Interview with David Hume, Esq." In *Dialogues Concerning Natural Religion*, by David Hume, 76–79. Edited with an introduction by Norman Kemp Smith. Library of Liberal Arts 174. Indianapolis: Bobbs-Merrill Educational, 1947.

Buckley, Cara. "Man Is Rescued by Stranger on Subway Tracks." *New York Times*, January 3, 2007, A1. http://www.nytimes.com/2007/01/03/nyregion/03life.html?_r=0/.

Darwin, Charles. *Descent of Man*. In *Darwin*. Edited by Robert Maynard Hutchins. Great Books of the Western World 49. Chicago: Encyclopedia Britannica, 1952.

———. *The Expression of Emotions in Man and Animals*. London: Murray, 1872.

———. *Origin of Species*. In *Darwin*. Edited by Robert Maynard Hutchins. Great Books of the Western World 49. Chicago: Encyclopedia Britannica, 1952.

Dawkins, Richard. *The Selfish Gene*. 30th anniversary ed. Oxford: Oxford University Press, 2006.

Descartes, René. "Early Writings." In *The Philosophical Writings of Descartes*, 1:2–5. Translated by John Cottingham et al. 3 vols. Cambridge: Cambridge University Press, 1984.

———. *Meditations on First Philosophy*. In *The Philosophical Writings of Descartes*, 2:3–383. 3 vols. Translated by John Cottingham et al. Cambridge: Cambridge University Press, 1984.

———. *Principles of Philosophy*. In *The Philosophical Writings of Descartes*, 1:177–291. Translated by John Cottingham et al. 3 vols. Cambridge: Cambridge University Press, 1984.

———. "Third Replies (to Hobbes)." In *The Philosophical Writings of Descartes*, 2:121–37. Translated by John Cottingham et al. 3 vols. Cambridge: Cambridge University Press, 1984.

Einstein, Albert. "The World as I See It." In *Ideas and Opinions*, 8–11. Translated by Sonja Bargmann. New York: Modern Library, 1994.

Feuerbach, Ludwig. *Principles of the Philosophy of the Future*. Translated by Manfred H. Vogel. Indianapolis: Hackett, 1986.

Hawking, Stephen, and Leonard Mlodinow. *The Grand Design*. New York: Bantam, 2010.

Heidegger, Martin. *Basic Questions in Philosophy*. Translated by Richard Rojcewicz and André Schuwer. Studies in Continental Thought. Bloomington: Indiana University Press, 1994.

———. *Being and Time*. Translated by John Macquarrie and Edward Robinson. New York: Harper, 1962.

———. "Letter on Humanism." In *Basic Writings*, edited by David Farrell Krell, 217–65. Rev. ed. San Francisco: HarperSanFrancisco, 1993.

———. "The Thing." In *Poetry, Language, Thought*, 161–84. Translated by Albert Hofstadter. New York: Harper & Row, 1971.

———. *Zollikon Seminars*. Edited by Medard Boss. Translated by Franz Mayr and Richard Askay. SPEP Studies in Historical Philosophy. Evanston, IL: Northwestern University Press, 2001.

Homer. *The Iliad*. Translated by Richmond Lattimore. Chicago: University of Chicago Press, 1951.

Hume, David. *A Treatise on Human Nature*, 2nd ed. Edited by L. A. Selby-Bigge. Oxford: Oxford University Press, 1978.

Husserl, Edmund. *Ideas I*. Translated by Fred Kersten. Dordrecht: Kluwer Academic, 1998.

Huxley, Aldous. *Brave New World, and Brave New World Revisited*. New York: HarperCollins, 2004.

Kahn, Charles H., ed. and trans. *The Art and Thought of Heraclitus*. Cambridge: Cambridge University Press, 1979.

Kahney, Leander. "The Ten Commandments of Steve." *Newsweek*. September 5, 2011.

Kant, Immanuel. "Conjectural Beginning of Human History." In *Toward Perpetual Peace and Other Writings on Politics, Peace, and History*, edited by Pauline Klengeld, 24–36. Translated by David L. Colclasure. Rethinking the Western Tradition. New Haven: Yale University Press, 2006.

———. *Critique of Practical Reason*. Translated by Werner S. Pluhar. Indianapolis: Hackett, 2002.

———. *Grounding for the Metaphysics of Morals; with, On a Supposed Right to Lie because of Philanthropic Concerns*. Translated by James W. Ellington. 3rd ed. Indianapolis: Hackett, 1993.

———. *Prolegomena to Any Future Metaphysics*. Translated by Paul Carus rev. by James W. Ellington. 2nd ed. Indianapolis: Hackett, 2001.

Kierkegaard, Søren. *Concluding Unscientific Postscript*. Translated by David Swenson. Princeton: Princeton University Press, 1941.

———. *A Kierkegaard Anthology*. Edited by Robert Bretall. Princeton: Princeton University Press, 1946.

———. *Works of Love*. Edited and translated by Howard V. Hong and Edna H. Hong. Kierkegaard's Writings 16. Princeton: Princeton University Press, 1995.

Kirk, G. S. et al. *The Presocratic Philosophers*. 2nd ed. Cambridge: Cambridge University Press, 1983.

Lévinas, Emmanuel. *Totality and Infinity: An Essay on Exteriority*. Translated by Alphonso Lingis. Duquesne Studies. Philosophical Series 24. Pittsburgh: Duquesne University Press, 1969.

Madison, Laurel. "Have We Been Careless with Socrates' Last Words? A Rereading of the *Phaedo*." *Journal of the History of Philosophy* 40 (2002) 421–36.

Marcel, Gabriel. "The Mystery of the Family." In *Homo Viator*, 68–97. Gloucester, MA: Smith, 1978.

Marion, Jean-Luc. *The Erotic Phenomenon*. Translated by Stephen E. Lewis. Chicago: University of Chicago Press, 2007.

Mill, John Stuart. *On Liberty*. Upper Saddle River, NJ: Prentice–Hall, 1997.

Nietzsche, Friedrich. *Beyond Good and Evil*. In *Basic Writings of Nietzsche*, edited and translated by Walter Kaufmann, 191–435. Modern Library of the World's Best Books. Modern Library Giants. New York: Modern Library, 1992.

———. *The Gay Science*. Translated by Walter Kaufmann. New York: Random House, 1974.

———. *Genealogy of Morals*. In *Basic Writings of Nietzsche*, edited and translated by Walter Kaufmann, 449–599. Modern Library of the World's Best Books. Modern Library Giants. New York: Modern Library, 1992.

———. *Philosophy in the Tragic Age of the Greeks*. Translated by Marianne Cowan. Gateway edition. Washington DC: Regnery, 1962.

Noë, Alva. *Out of Our Heads: Why You Are Not Your Brain, and Other Lessons from the Biology of Consciousness*. New York: Hill & Wang, 2009.

Pascal, Blaise. *Pensées*. Translated by A. J. Krailsheimer. Penguin Classics. London: Penguin, 1995.

Pico della Mirandola, Giovanni. *Oration on the Dignity of Man*. Translated by A. Robert Caponigri. Gateway edition. Washington DC: Regnery, 1956.

Pinker, Steven. "The Brain: The Mystery of Consciousness." *Time*. January 29, 2007. http://content.time.com/time/magazine/article/0,9171,1580394,00.html/.

———. *How the Mind Works*. New York: Norton, 1997.

Plato. *The Apology*. Translated by G. M. A. Grube. In *Plato: Complete Works*, edited by John M. Cooper, 17–36. Indianapolis: Hackett, 1997.

———. *Laws*. Translated by Trevor Saunders. In *Plato: Complete Works*, edited by John M. Cooper, 1318–1616. Indianapolis: Hackett, 1997.

———. *Phaedo*. Translated by G. M. A. Grube. In *Plato: Complete Works*, edited by John M. Cooper, 49–100. Indianapolis: Hackett, 1997.

———. *Phaedrus*. Translated by Alexander Nehemas and Paul Woodruff. In *Plato: Complete Works*, edited by John M. Cooper, 506–56. Indianapolis: Hackett, 1997.

———. *Republic*. Translated by G. M. A. Grube. Revised by C. D. C. Reeve. In *Plato: Complete Works*, edited by John M. Cooper, 971–1223. Indianapolis: Hackett, 1997.

———. *Symposium*. Translated by Alexander Nehemas and Paul Woodruff. In *Plato: Complete Works*, edited by John M. Cooper, 457–505. Indianapolis, IN: Hackett, 1997.

———. *Theaetetus*. Translated by M. J. Levett, revised by Myles Burnyeat. In *Plato: Complete Works*, edited by John M. Cooper, 157–234. Indianapolis: Hackett, 1997.

Plotinus. *The Essential Plotinus*. Translated by Elmer O'Brien, SJ. Indianapolis: Hackett, 1964.

Pope, Alexander. "Essay on Criticism." In *The Poetical Works of Alexander Pope*, edited by Adolphus William Ward, 51–71. New York: Crowell, 1896.

Rousseau, Jean-Jacques. *Discourse on the Origin of Inequality*. Translated by Donald A. Cress. Indianapolis: Hackett, 1992.

Russell, Bertrand. "The Existence of God—A Debate." In *A Modern Introduction to Philosophy*, edited by Paul Edwards and Arthur Pap, 473–90. New York: Free Press, 1965.

———. "A Free Man's Worship." In *Philosophy in the Twentieth Century: An Anthology*, edited by William Barrett and Henry D. Aiken, 2:703–9. 4 vols. New York: Random House, 1962.

———. *The Problems of Philosophy*. London: Oxford University Press, 1946.

Safer, Morley. "The Flavorists: Tweaking Tastes and Creating Cravings." *60 Minutes*. Nov. 27, 2011, http://www.cbsnews.com/news/the-flavorists-tweaking-tastes-and-creating-cravings-27-11-2011/.

Sample, Ian. "Stephen Hawking: 'There Is No Heaven; It's a Fairy Story.'" *The Guardian*. 15 May 2011, http://www.guardian.co.uk/science/2011/may/15/stephen-hawking-interview-there-is-no-heaven/.

Sartre, Jean-Paul. "Existentialism." Translated by Benard Frechtman. In *Existentialism and Human Emotions*, 9–51. Secaucus, NJ: Carol, 1993.

Scheler, Max. *Ressentiment*. Translated by Lewis B. Coser and William W. Holdheim. Marquette Studies in Philosophy 4. Milwaukee: Marquette University Press, 1994.

Searle, John R. *Mind, Language, and Society: Philosophy in the Real World*. New York: Basic Books, 1998.

Shakespeare, William. *Love Sonnets*. London: Phoenix, 1996.

Shoda, Yuichi et al. "Predicting Adolescent Cognitive and Self-Regulatory Competencies from Preschool Delay of Gratification: Identifying Diagnostic Conditions." *Developmental Psychology* 26 (1990) 978–86.

Thomas, Aquinas, Saint. *Summa Theologiae*. Translated by English Dominicans. New York: Benzinger, 1947.

Thoreau, Henry David. "Life without Principle." In *Walden and Other Writings*, 349–68. New York: Barnes & Noble, 1993.

———. *Walden*. In *Walden and Other Writings*, 3–275. New York: Barnes & Noble, 1993.

United States Supreme Court. *Planned Parenthood of Southeastern Pennsylvania v. Casey*. 505 U.S. 833 (1992).

Watterson, Bill. "Calvin and Hobbes." December 21, 1987. http://www.amureprints.com/reprints (ID 67209).

———. "Calvin and Hobbes." December 23, 1987. http://www.amureprints.com/reprints/ (ID 67211).

Wittgenstein, Ludwig. *On Certainty*. Edited by G. E. M. Anscombe and G. H. von Wright. Translated by Denis Paul and G. E. M. Anscombe. New York: Harper, 1969.

———. *Culture and Value*. Edited by G. H. von Wright. Translated by Peter Winch. Chicago: University of Chicago Press, 1980.

———. *Zettel*. Edited by G. E. M. Anscombe and G. H. von Wright. Translated by G. E. M. Anscombe. Berkeley: University of California Press, 1967.

CPSIA information can be obtained
at www.ICGtesting.com
Printed in the USA
LVHW091557180721
693026LV00002B/204